AF207232

Turning Twelve or More
Living by
The Articles of Faith

Happy 12th
Birthay
chantal

na n a

Turning Twelve or More
Living by
The Articles of Faith

Elaine Cannon

Bookcraft
Salt Lake City, Utah

Copyright © 1990 by Bookcraft, Inc.

All rights reserved. No part of this book may be reproduced in any form or by any means without permission in writing from the publisher, Bookcraft, Inc., 1848 West 2300 South, Salt Lake City, Utah 84119.

Bookcraft is a registered trademark of Bookcraft, Inc.

Library of Congress Catalog Card Number: 90–80495

ISBN 0–88494–732–7

First Printing, 1990

Printed in the United States of America

To Russell Orton, Cory Maxwell, Carrie Henderson, and Briton

Contents

Contents

The Articles of Faith
of The Church of Jesus Christ
# of Latter-day Saints

1. We believe in God, the Eternal Father, and in His Son, Jesus Christ, and in the Holy Ghost.

2. We believe that men will be punished for their own sins, and not for Adam's transgression.

3. We believe that through the Atonement of Christ, all mankind may be saved, by obedience to the laws and ordinances of the Gospel.

4. We believe that the first principles and ordinances of the Gospel are: first, Faith in the Lord Jesus Christ; second, Repentance; third, Baptism by immersion for the remission of sins; fourth, Laying on of hands for the gift of the Holy Ghost.

5. We believe that a man must be called of God, by prophecy, and by the laying on of hands by those who are in authority, to preach the Gospel and administer in the ordinances thereof.

6. We believe in the same organization that existed in the Primitive Church, namely, apostles, prophets, pastors, teachers, evangelists, and so forth.

7. We believe in the gift of tongues, prophecy, revelation, visions, healing, interpretation of tongues, and so forth.

8. We believe the Bible to be the word of God as far as it is translated correctly; we also believe the Book of Mormon to be the word of God.

9. We believe all that God has revealed, all that He does now reveal, and we believe that He will yet reveal many great and important things pertaining to the Kingdom of God.

10. We believe in the literal gathering of Israel and in the restoration of the Ten Tribes; that Zion (the New Jerusalem) will be built upon the American continent; that Christ will reign personally upon the earth; and, that the earth will be renewed and receive its paradisiacal glory.

11. We claim the privilege of worshiping Almighty God according to the dictates of our own conscience, and allow all men the same privilege, let them worship how, where, or what they may.

12. We believe in being subject to kings, presidents, rulers, and magistrates, in obeying, honoring, and sustaining the law.

13. We believe in being honest, true, chaste, benevolent, virtuous, and in doing good to all men; indeed, we may say that we follow the admonition of Paul—We believe all things, we hope all things, we have endured many things, and hope to be able to endure all things. If there is anything virtuous, lovely, or of good report or praiseworthy, we seek after these things.

(Articles of Faith 1:1–13.)

1

Turning Twelve or More

Are you eleven going on twelve?

Twelve turning teenager?

Maybe you are fourteen going on grown-up.

This book is for you!

Turning twelve is a turning point. It changes life for a girl or boy. It is the giant step into another world. For one thing, it is out of Primary and into Aaronic Priesthood* for boys. And it is so-long, Merrie Miss, and hello, Young Women, for the girls.

Turning twelve brings new responsibilities. Some of these things have to do with all the rest of your life on earth—even beyond!

---

*Sometimes in this book you will see an asterisk (*) after a word or term. If you want to know what the word before the asterisk means, look the word up at the back of the book in the chapter called "What the Words Mean."

Jake and Casey, who were turning twelve next year, were doing their annual Christmas checkout at the super-store in their town. They were on their own, casing the place to see the new merchandise put there to please boys their age at Christmastime.

"Hey, Casey, over here!" Jake called to his friend, and he held up a pair of ski boots handsome enough to make a guy forget all his troubles. "Look at these babies! Wow! Say, Casey, do you still believe in Santa Claus?"

"If I say yes, will I get the ski boots for Christmas?" retorted Casey.

The boys had been asking each other this question annually. Wishing and wondering about Santa Claus is, after all, a magical pursuit. It is an idea that seems to make Christmas more surprising. So when Jake asked Casey if he still believed in Santa, it was more to build a mood than to get information.

They were thoughtful for a few moments, absorbed in the abundance of another season of wanting and wishing, getting and giving.

Casey picked up a computer space toy that was currently being advertised on television. It was one of those "grown-up toys" that he'd been wanting for a long time. He knew his dad would like it too. He turned it over in his hands, examining it thoughtfully before putting it down. Then suddenly he spoke. "Jake, do you believe in visitors from other planets, the kind that would come in a UFO or a gizmo like this thing?" He held up the toy for Jake to see.

"Do I believe in space people? I dunno. What does that have to do with Christmas, anyway?"

"Something, I guess," replied Casey. "Remember our lesson at church last week? Christmas is about God, and we learned that God was the Creator of the universe and everything in it. So, do you believe *that*?"

"Of course I believe *that*," Jake said. Turning to Casey, he asked, "Have *you* ever wondered about all this—God, creation, the universe, space people, earth people . . . us?"

Casey moved over to the display of small telescopes, magnifying glasses, binoculars, and microscopes. "Just because we haven't seen the planet Uranus doesn't mean it isn't out there,'' Casey said, gazing at the ceiling with a pair of binoculars.

''Like Santa Claus?'' laughed Jake, picking up a big magnifying lens and peering closely at Casey.

''Oh, come off it, Sherlock!''

''Just trying to see if you're really there, Casey.'' Jake laughingly punched his friend in the arm. ''Well, I guess we don't always have to see something before we can believe it's there. Like germs, for example. We can't see them, but we know they're there. They're responsible for that flu you had last week, for instance.''

''Right,'' agreed Casey. ''It's like your bedroom in the dark. You know that all your stuff is still around you, even if you can't see it.''

''Deep talk, Casey,'' said Jake. ''Good idea. Well, I have to get home.''

That night Dad and Jake were working on a Christmas project together. Jake was thinking about his conversation with Casey that afternoon. He told his dad about it and then asked, ''Dad, I guess you've never seen God, have you?''

''No.''

''But you believe in God. Is it hard for you to believe in God when you can't see him?''

''Not at all,'' his father replied, energetically pushing another sparkler into place on one of the Yule logs they were making as gifts for neighbors. ''Jake, even if I were blind and couldn't see anything at all, I would know that God lives. I talk to him in prayer. We talk to him as a family through prayer.''

''OK. But, Dad, why do you suppose we can't see him?''

''Oh, maybe we aren't pure enough. Maybe we have to learn more. Maybe he wants us to have stronger faith.* Maybe face-to-face seeing at this time is for prophets.''

''Yes, Dad, I know we pray, but how do we know he is there listening?''

---

*See ''What the Words Mean.''

"Because we get answers to our prayers. You know that. We have felt his Spirit with us too." Jake's dad scrunched the staple gun against the last piece of holly and secured it on the Yule log. Then he said, "Jake, I have a good idea. Why don't you take the assignment for family home evening next Monday? We'll talk about this some more. There's a little story on the subject that may help the younger children understand that seeing is not always necessary for believing. I'll find it for you."

At family home evening Jake read from the manual the story of the little boy who prayed before bedtime, with his mother sitting nearby, quietly listening. After the prayer she tucked him into bed with a goodnight kiss. As she turned off the light the little boy said, "I don't like it when the light is off, Mommy. I can't see you!"

She stood there silently a moment.

"Mommy, are you still there?"

"Yes, Stephen, I'm still here. And that's how it is with Heavenly Father. You can't see him, but if you keep very still and reach for him with your heart, you will know in your heart and in your mind that he is there—just as you know that I'm here even if I'm very quiet. Even if it's dark and you can't see me."

"Oh!"

Stephen's mother leaned over and kissed the little boy on the forehead. "There. You know I am here even if you can't see me. Think about this while you sleep, dear one."

Jake continued his family home evening lesson by having family members sit quietly with their eyes shut. Then he said, "Often our emotions or our sense of feeling lets us know things first. You know that Mom and Dad are in the room, even if you can't see them. You sense each other's presence. Well, when we pray, we can know that God is there if we concentrate on him instead of letting the mind wander. When we stop to think, read, and feel, we know that our spirit self is a child of God. Actually, we're not only in the same family here on earth; we're all part of Heavenly Father's family too."

It was a good lesson. Jake had prayed for guidance and had thought a lot about these things as he prepared. He felt good as he led the discussion. When the family knelt in a circle at the close of family home evening, a wonderful thing happened. Everyone felt close to Heavenly Father. Each one, for that moment, knew that God lived and was listening while they talked with him.

It was wonderful.

Whether we are twelve or more, it is true that if we seek God and worship him, follow his principles for the good life, and live by the Articles of Faith,* we can know joy.

We say that we believe in God. And we do! We believe that God sent his Firstborn Son to earth with a mission to further his work, which is "to bring to pass the immortality* and eternal life"* of mankind (see Moses 1:39).

We have learned this:

—From our parents.

—From our Church meetings and classes.

—From personal study of the scriptures.

—From talking with others who truly understand.

—From the promptings of the Holy Ghost.

We believe these things because we have been taught to be true believers. And through believing, an act of faith, we receive great blessings. After faith come the miracles,* on a grander or lesser scale according to our needs and readiness.

We believe in God, even though we can't see him, because we can see all that he has created—every mountain, every river, the roaring ocean, the whispering, tall trees, every quiet creature below, every star above, each fragrant flower, all the colorful vegetables and fruits, and each marvelous human being.

We believe in God because we can close our eyes and reverently let our inner self draw close to him. When we do this he keeps his promise and draws close to us.

---

*See "What the Words Mean."

We believe in God because the scriptures remind us that the Spirit itself bears witness with our own spirit that we are the children of God (see Romans 8:16).

And we don't need a telescope or a magnifying glass to know this.

The thirteen Articles of Faith list some of the other good things we believe in.

How did they come to be?

2

How the Articles of Faith Came to Be

Before you learn exactly how the Articles of Faith came to be, it will help you if you understand how God works when he wants his children on earth to learn something important for their day.

For example, each year as you go back to school you wonder who your teachers will be. So much of what you learn—and how much you like class—depends on the teacher. Each teacher is prepared for a particular subject. Since you know this you are mentally ready to be taught a certain subject by a certain teacher. You don't expect to learn advanced math from the sewing instructor or the band leader. And you wouldn't expect to learn God's truth from someone who wasn't a student of the gospel* or

*See "What the Words Mean."

who didn't love Heavenly Father and Jesus enough to do their work.

Each good teacher is a kind of specialist.

Prophets* of God always have been specialists too. Prophets are teachers for God among his children on earth. Prophets have an important mission, and the mission of each one is a little different from that of the others. Looking back over the history of God's prophets, we can see this, and we can also see where the Articles of Faith fit.

Noah, one of God's greatest prophets, lived four thousand years ago. What he did then is still important to us today. He came to earth at a time when people were very wicked. They wanted to do what *they* wanted to do more than they wanted to obey God's will.* Their lives were so full of mistakes and impurities that they no longer had the Holy Spirit with them. They would not listen to God's prophet, Noah.

God became angry. He told Noah that he was going to send a mighty flood to cleanse the earth of evil. He asked Noah to build an ark that would float on the flood waters. Noah was to fill this ark with obedient people and with animals and plants—male and female and all varieties—to start earth life over again after the flood. And that is what happened.

Noah was a great prophet who talked with God and obeyed him. It's a good thing he did, isn't it?

Moses was a wonderful prophet too.

Moses was a specialist in leading people.

Moses came to earth at a time when the Israelites were slaves to their enemies, who were cruel and who loved war and wealth. The Israelites' enemies were full of wicked desires and made other people live like animals. God gave Moses the Ten Commandments, and Moses gave them to the people to help them live better lives.

Since the beginning of time God has worked through prophets to help people become perfected and learn how to avoid destruction. Adam was a prophet. Abraham was a prophet. Lehi was a prophet. Isaiah was a prophet. Alma was a prophet. Noah

---

*See ''What the Words Mean.''

and Moses were prophets. And Joseph Smith was a prophet. Each had a different specialty to serve both God and their fellowmen. Joseph's was to bring about the restoration of the gospel.

Now let's find out how the Articles of Faith came to be.

Before the restoration* of the Church of Jesus Christ in 1830, people didn't know what they needed to know to get back into the presence of Heavenly Father. They didn't have the full truth. Good people were looking for help.

This was a worry to Joseph Smith. He read the Bible as a young boy. When he was just fourteen years old, he earnestly prayed for help. His prayers were answered in a wondrous way— Heavenly Father and Jesus appeared to him and talked with him and taught him. Jesus told him that none of the churches were teaching the truth about God. Joseph was to restore order and truth so people would learn how to be close to God.

Because Joseph's mission was such a remarkable one, it interested many people of his day. What was different about this new religion? What did Joseph Smith teach? Why did people follow him? What did the Mormons believe in? Many people wanted to know.

In the early 1840s a Mr. Bastow was planning to write a history of the state of New Hampshire. There were members of The Church of Jesus Christ of Latter-day Saints, known as Mormons, living in that state, but people didn't seem to know much about what they believed, because the Church had only been an organization for a very few years. Mr. Bastow wanted to find out more about these people and their beliefs, and apparently he contacted his friend John Wentworth, a newspaper editor in Chicago, to get information.

Even this important editor didn't know much about the Mormons, so he decided to write to the Prophet Joseph and ask him. Joseph Smith answered the request in what has become known as the Wentworth Letter, one of the most important documents in Church literature. The last part of this important

---

*See "What the Words Mean."

letter was a summary of some of the doctrines* of the Church. We now call this summary the Articles of Faith.

The Wentworth Letter was published in March 1842 in the Church newspaper, *Times and Seasons.* The Articles of Faith were included in the Pearl of Great Price, which was accepted as a standard work of the Church at the general conference* of October 1880.

We talked about school teachers being specialists. We discussed prophets being specialists. What about you and your special contribution?

Now that you are growing up you will begin to make serious preparations so that someday you will have a career or a profession —a way to earn a living. You will hope to excel at something in particular. You will become a specialist in something.

Preparing for a sound future is important. You will want to have a patriarchal blessing* as part of this preparation. You will want to know whether at that point Heavenly Father has something to say to you about your particular mission.

You may or may not become a prophet—or the wife of a prophet, who helps a prophet serve God. Through this blessing, however, you may learn why you have been sent to earth at this particular time and for what special service.

In addition to the career you choose, there may be something that only you can do in the Lord's kingdom on earth to help people grow and to help them become worthy to live forever with Heavenly Father.

Joseph Smith, a prophet of God, a specialist in the work of the Lord on earth, was inspired to write the thirteen Articles of Faith. Ever since then members of The Church of Jesus Christ of Latter-day Saints have been taught to use the Articles of Faith as a guide in their lives.

There it is! You don't have to wait until ''someday.'' You can become a specialist *right now* in living by the Articles of Faith and in helping others do so too.

---

*See ''What the Words Mean.''

3

Learning the Articles of Faith

Here is a riddle for you:

Q.   Why is a preacher like a camel?

A.   Because he goes on and on and never knows how dry he
     is.

An eleven-year-old named Karen shared that riddle when she
was trying to memorize the Articles of Faith before graduation
from Primary. She said the Articles of Faith were like the preacher
and the camel—dry and boring!

Karen's family had all been baptized into the Church in the
past year, and she had a lot of catching up to do. The other
children had been learning the Articles of Faith right along, but
here she was a new member of the Church and had so many
things to learn that the thirteen statements of belief seemed to her
hard, long, and, yes, dry and boring.

The missionaries* who taught Karen's family the gospel had worked with her and helped her some. But still there was a lot to learn when you never have heard anything about Mormons.

One day Karen, riding home on the school bus, sat next to Amy, who was memorizing a part for the school play. Amy not only had to memorize a lot of lines but she also had to remember when to say those lines and where to stand and what to do when she said them during the performance. Just like a movie star or a character in a TV program!

Since Amy was busy with her own work and didn't seem anxious to have company, Karen decided to move next to someone who would talk to her. But then she thought of her Articles of Faith project and stayed instead to watch Amy as she memorized her lines.

Karen sat very quietly, so as not to disturb Amy.

Karen soon became fascinated with this process of memorizing. She noticed that Amy had printed on a separate card each speech she had to make. She would try to have a certain part of it memorized before the bus had traveled one block or made the next stop. If there was time when the bus stopped, she would repeat the whole part she had memorized. When the bus started up again, she would work on a new part. Amy often repeated the words in rhythm with the turning bus wheels.

So Amy has a system, Karen thought. Maybe that system would help Karen memorize the Articles of Faith. If she knew them by heart she could repeat them when she was trying to help her friends understand what members of the Church believed in.

She'd start with Amy.

When they came to the end of the bus trip, Karen asked Amy if Amy could come over some day soon after school and explain her method of memorizing. She told Amy she had something she wanted to memorize too. She suggested that maybe they could help each other.

And they did.

---

*See "What the Words Mean."

Later Amy went to Karen's home, and they worked together—Amy memorizing her part in the play and Karen memorizing the Articles of Faith. They coached each other and tested each other. They worked hard and had fun too.

It was worth those hours of work. Amy was terrific in the play and didn't muff her lines at all. Karen memorized the Articles of Faith and found that they were not dry (like a camel or the old preacher). And another wonderful thing happened too. Each time they got together to work on the memorizing, Karen answered Amy's questions about the Church and about what she believed. They became best friends.

Of course, the best part of the story is that one day Amy was baptized and confirmed a member of the Church!

Here are some suggestions for memorizing.

1. Do it! Quit putting it off.

2. Study the text. Make sense of what you are trying to memorize. Notice how each part fits in with the rest.

3. Search the meaning. Try to understand what you are memorizing.

4. Repeat each part over and over. Every time you start a new part, repeat what you already have learned. You'll learn the material, at last, as a whole.

5. Think! Concentrate! Focus! Control yourself so that you can zero in on what you are doing. What you put into a computer is what comes out. Your mind is a computer. Fuzzy commands on the computer make fuzzy performance.

6. Find time. Make time, if you have to, when you can work undisturbed—with no TV, music, chores, family, or friendly interference. Maybe you can work when you're on the school bus in your own seat. Maybe you can work at night before you go to sleep. Maybe you can set your alarm and beat the family out of bed. You can have quiet time then to accomplish a lot of things you want to.

7. Pray for help. Ask Heavenly Father, in the name of Jesus Christ, for the power of the Holy Ghost. Heaven will help you. You'll see.

There is one suggestion for remembering the Articles of Faith that comes from the Primary Association. You probably learned this as a younger child. That system is that each article has a key word to give you a clue and help you recall the whole statement. These are the key words that the children learn in Primary:

1. Godhead	6. Organization	11. We claim
2. Men	7. Gifts	12. Law
3. Atonement	8. Translate	13. Admonition
4. First Principles	9. Revelation	
5. Hands	10. Ten Tribes	

The key words we will use in this book are somewhat different. They are as follows:

1. Godhead	6. Organization	11. Worship
2. Agency	7. Gifts	12. Law
3. Atonement	8. Scriptures	13. Seek
4. Principles	9. Revelation	
5. Hands	10. Gathering	

You may want to make a list of your own key words:

1.	6.	11.
2.	7.	12.
3.	8.	13.
4.	9.	
5.	10.	

When you are trying to understand the Articles of Faith that you are memorizing, it helps to do some scripture* study on each one. You probably know how to look up a written scriptural reference. But just in case you have forgotten, this is the way to go about it.

---

*See "What the Words Mean."

Find the volume—the Book of Mormon,* the Bible (with the Old Testament and the New Testament), the Doctrine and Covenants, and the Pearl of Great Price.*

Next you look up the "book" in that volume, or the chapter or section in the volume, and then the verse.

For example, sometimes this abbreviation is used for Doctrine and Covenants scriptures: D&C 88:86. This scriptural reference will be found in the volume called the Doctrine and Covenants, the eighty-eighth section, verse eighty-six.

Another example is Mosiah 13:20. This scriptural reference will be found in the volume called the Book of Mormon, in the book named Mosiah, in the thirteenth chapter, verse twenty.

Sometimes there will be more than one book of the same name in a volume, and so there will be a number in front of the name. For example, 3 Nephi, 1 Corinthians, 2 Peter, and so on.

Later in this book, at the end of the discussion of each Article of Faith, there will be some scriptural references which can help you understand it better.

The Articles of Faith are scripture. They are included in the Pearl of Great Price. You'll find that book after the Doctrine and Covenants. Not everything we believe is stated in the thirteen Articles of Faith. One of the articles reminds us that God "will yet reveal many great and important things."

These thirteen statements are basic to our belief, however. When you learn them you will want to live by them. Let them be a guide to your life-style, your choices, your appearance, your thinking, and the language you use—and don't use! Let them strengthen your faith and direct your prayers.

Little by little, line upon line, you can learn what God wants you to know so that you'll be happy on earth and pure enough to live with him in heaven.

Here is something else you can do besides memorize the thirteen Articles of Faith. You can refresh your memory (your computer mind) by reading again Joseph Smith's own story about

---

*See "What the Words Mean."

his experience as a fourteen-year-old boy. It is wonderful reading. You will enjoy it. For example, here is a quote from the Pearl of Great Price, Joseph Smith—History 1:25.

"I had actually seen a light, and in the midst of that light I saw two Personages, and they did in reality speak to me; and though I was hated and persecuted for saying that I had seen a vision, yet it was true; and while they were persecuting me, reviling me, and speaking all manner of evil against me falsely for so saying, I was led to say in my heart: Why persecute me for telling the truth? I have actually seen a vision*; and who am I that I can withstand God, or why does the world think to make me deny what I have actually seen? For I had seen a vision; I knew it, and I knew that God knew it, and I could not deny it, neither dared I do it; at least I knew that by so doing I would offend God, and come under condemnation.*"

You owe so much to Joseph Smith! Under the Lord's direction, in courage and faithfulness he established The Church of Jesus Christ of Latter-day Saints so that we can learn the full truth about God, Jesus, and the Holy Ghost. You can read the Book of Mormon, which the Prophet Joseph miraculously translated. You can learn about the plan of life* and the truth about yourself and your relationship to God. You can learn the Articles of Faith and try to live by them.

---

*See "What the Words Mean."

4

The Thirteen Articles of Faith

In this chapter we will look at all of the Articles of Faith, one by one, and see how they can be applied to daily living.

Read the story that illustrates each Article of Faith, and then read the section entitled ''What Does This Mean to You?'' As you read you will discover how these thirteen important statements of belief relate to you directly, and you will learn various ways in which you can make them a part of your life.

Also included are lists of scriptures you can read to better understand the principles taught in each Article of Faith.

1. We believe in God, the Eternal Father, and in His Son, Jesus Christ, and in the Holy Ghost.

About the First Article of Faith: Godhead

We'll call him Daniel (like Daniel in the Old Testament) because he was such a good and faithful boy. He believed in praying to Heavenly Father. He believed in God. He believed in prayers being answered. This is his story.

Daniel and his mother had gone to the hospital to see her brother Wayne, who had suffered a dreadful accident. His head was badly injured, and Daniel's mother was certain Wayne was going to die. She wept and worried as she and Daniel sat together in the hospital room waiting for the sick relative to be brought back from surgery.

"Don't worry, Mother," comforted Daniel. "I'll talk to Heavenly Father." Daniel knelt by the side of the empty bed near the chair where his mother sat. He began to pray, and it sounded as if he were having a gentle conversation face to face with God.

He explained the situation and then he concluded the short prayer by saying, "Heavenly Father, this sick man is my favorite uncle, and we need him so much. Please make him well. You can. I know you can!"

There were a few moments of silence and then Daniel said, "OK. Thanks."

Daniel rose from his knees and explained to his mother, "Heavenly Father said OK. He'll make Uncle Wayne well. Maybe you'd better stop crying now."

Daniel's mother was touched by his faith and confidence in God, but she was concerned that Daniel's faith would fail if things didn't turn out exactly the way he wanted—if Wayne died. She dabbed at her eyes with tissue and talked slowly and carefully. "Daniel, I'm sure that Heavenly Father loves Uncle Wayne and you. But maybe God has something else in mind other than a healing blessing. After all, this serious accident may be Heavenly Father's way of getting Uncle Wayne back into His presence. We all have to die sometime," she finished sadly.

"Mother, I told you Heavenly Father said OK—and that means that Uncle Wayne will be OK," reminded Daniel firmly.

And he was.

Later, when Uncle Wayne's doctor heard the story about Daniel's faith and prayers, he said, "Well, I know that Daniel's prayers were answered. I was the attending physician. I sewed Wayne all around his head. I know how bad it was. Only God could have kept that man alive."

For Daniel, believing in God meant that he could talk with Heavenly Father in the name of Jesus Christ and through the power of the Holy Ghost. Oh, yes, Daniel was a true believer.

Daniel lived by the first Article of Faith, didn't he?

The first Article of Faith is very important because it declares that you and I and other members of the Church believe in a Godhead* with three separate beings known as Heavenly Father,*

---

*See "What the Words Mean."

his Son Jesus Christ,* and the Holy Ghost.* That knowledge brings blessings to our lives.

Whether or not anybody believes in God, he is still there. He is their Father in Heaven. Everyone who comes to earth was first a spiritual child of God, our Heavenly Father.

What Does This Mean to You?

It means that if you learn and live by the Articles of Faith you will:

1. Have greater happiness.
2. Have fewer problems.
3. Handle life's challenges better.
4. Become more like Jesus.
5. Become prepared to live in heaven in the presence of Heavenly Father and Jesus for all eternity.
6. Be able to effectively help friends and family members understand sacred* truths about the Godhead, their plan of life for us, and the principles we should live by.
7. Notice that earth seems to become more and more like what you think heaven must be.
8. Want to talk with God through prayer more frequently and fervently. What a difference that can make in life while you are growing up and growing older and getting ready to return to Heavenly Father someday.

When President Benson was about your age, he memorized a verse which he has recited on many occasions over the years. It is a good one that you might memorize too.

> I know not by what methods rare
> But this I know, God answers prayer.
> I know that He has given His word,
> Which tells me prayer is always heard,
> And will be answered, soon or late.

---

*See "What the Words Mean."

And so I pray and calmly wait.
I know not if the blessing sought
Will come in just the way I thought;
But leave my prayers with Him alone,
Whose will is wiser than my own,
Assured that He will grant my quest,
Or send some answer far more blessed.

(Eliza M. Hickok, ''Prayer'')

It means that you, too, can know that God lives. He loves you. He will answer your prayers according to what he, your Creator, knows is best for you.

And because you know these things, you can help others understand them. So it is a good idea to follow Paul's advice to Timothy and live as ''an example of the believers'' in the first Article of Faith: ''We believe in God, the Eternal Father, and in His Son, Jesus Christ, and in the Holy Ghost.''

Scriptures to Study

Bible: Matthew 3:16–17; Mark 9:7
Book of Mormon: 3 Nephi 11:25
Doctrine and Covenants 130:22–23

2.   We believe that men will be punished for their own sins, and not for Adam's transgression.

About the Second Article of Faith: Agency

Josh's ski-burned face was all smiles as Sister Delaney began to wrap up her Sunday School lesson on choice* and consequences.* Josh liked what he was hearing.

Sister Delaney was grateful to have Josh's full attention, for a change. He was a fine skier and put the sport before almost everything. He had a battle with skiing and the Sabbath day. He'd rather be skiing. If he did show up in class, he was thinking skiing and practicing skiing moves from his chair. Head dipped, shoulders shaped over, knees close together one way, hips swiveled the other. Back and forth, all the time she was talking!

However, this time Josh was listening. This time maybe he'd learn something that would give church the cutting edge over Sunday skiing.

Sister Delaney continued: "Free agency* is the right to act for yourself."

---

*See "What the Words Mean."

"All right! Yeah! Hey, I can do what I want, when I want!" Josh exploded before the rest of the class, enthusiastically pumping one arm up and down, doubling and flexing open his fingers. Then, slamming his hand against his neighbor's palm, he added, "Gimme five."

The room resounded with giggles. Some of the boys even joined in a kind of cheer for Josh. Agency sounded like the best thing to happen on earth since flip tops for soda pop cans.

"Sister Delaney, agency is the right to do or *not* do what we want—right?" asked Molly, looking over at the boys.

"Right! And let's hope you all use your free agency to do what is right."

Now the class was with her, and the questions popped.

"Sister Delaney, are you serious about this principle you've just been telling us about?"

"Yeah, is this for real?"

"Does it work for kids or just grown-ups?"

"Does the bishop* know about it?"

"How come parents weren't ever taught this?"

Now it was Sister Delaney's turn to smile. "The freedom to choose and act is God's gift to every person. God also has given us the gospel* to live by. If we haven't learned the gospel or if we *choose* to ignore it, we are often unhappy."

"I hate being unhappy," said Molly. "I guess that's why we come to church to learn how to choose."

"Well, that's surely one good reason," agreed Sister Delaney.

"My father says one man's free agency ends where the other fellow's nose begins," said Peter.

"My mother says that a girl's free agency ends where her sister's new blouse begins," added Mindy, providing something for the girls to think about.

"Good point!" said Sister Delaney. "But, you know, a girl is still free to try to wear her sister's new blouse without permission; a boy is still free to poke someone else in the nose. They can

---

*See "What the Words Mean."

choose to act that way. But if they do, what do you think happens?''

The class members talked among themselves a moment, some of them even testing the principle by putting a playful fist to the nose of the person sitting next to them.

Josh had an answer. ''Anybody who punches my nose gets punched back!''

The Sunday School class sounded their agreement. Some people clapped. One said, ''Sure, the person getting socked has free agency to hit back.''

''Now we're getting someplace. Your actions bring about certain results. When you act, someone else may react. When you make a choice, you also choose the consequences.''

''What do you mean, consequences?'' asked Josh.

Jeffrey spoke up. ''You poke someone in the nose and he pokes you back. Your nose bleeds. Maybe his does too. A bloody or hurt nose is the *consequence* of your act of aggression to a person's face.''

''All right,'' said Sister Delaney. ''Here is another example. If you choose to stay away from church, you probably won't know the gospel. You could make wrong choices all along the way in life. Those are the consequences of your free act of doing something else on Sunday instead of going to church.''

Josh got the message. He hung his head thoughtfully.

Sister Delaney felt it had been a good lesson.

Look over the following examples of choices and consequences. Maybe there is a message in them for you.

You see a traffic light up ahead. It is red. You can stop your bike or wheel through the red light. That light is there to protect you, but you have your free agency.

If you choose to study for the test, you will do better than if you choose not to study.

If you don't dress warmly for skiing, the consequences are that you are cold and miserable.

If you steal, you are a thief in trouble with the law.

Suppose you wear your sister's new blouse without her permission, and you tear it on your locker door. You'll have one angry sister, at least. Some consequences!

When your cousin isn't looking, you nudge his golf ball in the wrong direction, and someday he finds out that you are a poor sport. You aren't quite trusted anymore. These consequences of your choice are hard to change.

If you fool around with drugs and get hooked, your choice brings bitter problems or consequences.

As baptized and confirmed members of the Church, we learn and try to live by the second Article of Faith, which says, "We believe that men will be punished for their own sins, and not for Adam's transgression.*" Or Eve's, we might add.

You've heard about Adam and Eve living in a garden of great peace and beauty. Food came without much effort. Animals were tame. Nobody quarreled or got sick. Life was pleasant and easy. Imagine!

Of course, Adam and Eve weren't learning much.

Then they fell into temptation and had to suffer the consequences.

Some churches teach—and some people believe—that because Adam was the first man and he disobeyed Heavenly Father, all mankind is punished. Because Adam and Eve chose to use their free agency and succumb to temptation, some philosophies teach that we too are spoiled, soiled, or sinners. But we believe that each of us is punished for his own sins and not for Adam's or Eve's transgressions.

You need to remember that God told Adam and Eve to have children and replenish the earth. He also warned them that if they chose to eat of the forbidden fruit, life would be different. They would suffer the consequences. These consequences included being changed and being sent out of the lovely garden away from God. No longer did they enjoy peace and an easy life. Life was hard and full of challenges. No more talking with God face to face.

---

*See "What the Words Mean."

That separation from God's presence is called *spiritual death*. And since they had become mortal, they would also suffer *physical death.*

Adam and Eve's choice in the garden brought into play the Father's sacred plan of life.

We come to earth without flaws, without anybody else's sins on our backs. It is what *we* learn, what *we* do, and what *we* don't do that makes the difference, not what somebody else chooses to do or not do.

This idea, this knowledge, is exciting!

Let's talk about Josh again for a moment, to impress this idea on your mind. Josh, you see, can go skiing on Sunday and it won't be your problem. It will be Josh's. Missing church could mean he won't learn the will of God, he won't have the Spirit with him. Those are the consequences of his choosing Sunday skiing over Sunday School. But he is the loser—not you.

Sammy Linebaugh was the youth speaker on this subject in sacrament* meeting in the Arlington Hills Ward, Salt Lake Emigration Stake. She said:

"We all want to be happy. . . . One great means to happiness is the opportunity we have to exercise free agency.

"Consider the price that was paid to obtain this free agency. Before the Creation, Satan tried to persuade God to destroy the agency of man, as he said, 'Behold, here am I, send me, I will be thy son, and I will redeem all mankind, that one soul* shall not be lost' (Moses 4:1).

"Yet the Savior prevailed with his offer—that he would carry out the Father's plan, that we should be free to choose and thus free to fail. This allowed Adam and Eve the freedom to partake of the fruit and experience the consequences of having made that choice.

"As a result, this life is risky!

"That we are free to fail and succeed suggests two cautions:

"First, we should not allow ourselves to believe that because we are members of the kingdom of God on earth* we are exempt

---

*See "What the Words Mean."

28

from failure. The Father's plan for free agency allows all men the ability and choice to fail or succeed.

"The second concept to be aware of when we use our free agency is that we ought to want the consequences of the things we want. There is no such thing as freedom from consequences.

"To keep all the commandments and guidelines of the Church requires a sacrifice in one form or another by each of us. But it is this difficulty and sacrifice that separates us from the world and brings us closer to Heavenly Father. Reasons for which we may choose to break these rules may seem important at the time, but when we put into perspective all that we might be jeopardizing, those reasons seem terribly insufficient in comparison to the chance to live again with our Father in Heaven." (Used by permission.)

What Does This Mean to You?

It means that the second Article of Faith is an important reminder of the consequences of choice: each boy and girl, each man and woman, suffers for his or her own sins and not for Adam's transgression. You choose, but *you* pay for your mistakes or enjoy your wise choices.

It means that if your friend blew up a balloon and you poked it with a pin, a popped balloon (and a sad friend, no doubt!) would be the consequence of that unkind act.

You can do what you want, but there will be consequences— some good, some bad, depending on how you choose.

It's a good idea to be an "example of the believers" in the second Article of Faith, which says, "We believe that men will be punished for their own sins, and not for Adam's transgression."

Scriptures to Study

Bible: Galatians 6:7
Book of Mormon: Alma 30:8
Doctrine and Covenants 138:4
Pearl of Great Price: Abraham 3:24, 26

3. We believe that through the Atonement* of Christ, all mankind may be saved, by obedience to the laws and ordinances* of the Gospel.

About the Third Article of Faith: Atonement

For once everybody was at family home evening, including Grandma Egan.

But it hadn't been easy. Spring was such a busy time for school children, and each was involved in his or her own thing.

And yesterday it seemed as if Grandma Egan wouldn't be well enough to come. This morning they'd had a special family prayer for eighty-seven-year-old Grandma. Even though she felt miserable and was fragile, Grandma came for the special Easter family home evening. Their prayers had been answered.

As soon as Grandma was comfortable in the recliner chair, Dad sent Kevin after the rest of the family.

Kevin personally dragged Ben away from a video game. Ben joined Kevin because he enjoyed having the power of disturbing everyone's peace—making them do something they didn't think they wanted to do.

---

*See "What the Words Mean."

Together Kevin and Ben invaded Shelly's perfumed and private room. They skinnied past her easel, which held her precious project for art class. Knock that over, and Shelly not only would not come to family home evening but she might abandon the family forever—or at least two members of it. Kevin's manner was humble and pleading, flattering and grateful, while Ben acted as if he were going to be sick!

"Come with us, you gorgeous creature. Everything is better when you're there. Bless us with your presence, brilliant and beautiful older sister!"

It worked. Shelly came.

The three of them trooped to Elizabeth's room, where she was rearranging her Easter basket one more time and sneaking sweet nibbles along the way.

"Bring your fattest egg if you want to, but come along, Lizzie, my pal." Kevin changed his style with each one.

The four of them found Jason down in the basement with friends, working with their ham radio equipment. Nothing would persuade him to leave now—he made that known in an angry word battle.

"Jase, old pal," soothed Kevin, "remember you offered the prayer when we asked Heavenly Father to bless Grandma Egan? Well, your prayer was answered. She's here. You absolutely have to come. Say good-bye to your friends and fall in. Now!"

"Gig, Tony, Doug . . . sorry, I forgot, but tonight is special." Ben made a big bow, which Elizabeth imitated, and with a sweeping gesture ushered Jason's friends up the stairs ahead of him.

The brothers and sisters followed and quickly arrived at the family room, where Mother and Dad, Grandma, the toddler twins, and the new baby were waiting.

The table was decorated with their favorite Easter things. Just as always. Just the way they liked it.

There was the porcelain figure of Christ in Gethsemane, mounted on a revolving music box that played "As I Have Loved You." Aunt Gail had made it several years ago.

There was an Easter lily blooming among sprigs of forsythia. Magically, Mother had forced open the startling yellow flowers by soaking the stems in warm water for several days.

There was the precious ivory piece Dad had brought back from a museum in the East. It was a small version of Christ's descent from the cross, with tiny, intricately carved figures clamoring to release their beloved Jesus from the spikes that held his hands and feet to the timber.

There was the olive-wood bowl from Jerusalem filled with hand-painted ostrich eggs, symbol of new life.

There was the big hollow sugar egg, decorated with frosting ribbon, roses, and green leaves. Inside on green Easter grass was a tiny cutout photo of some of the children when they were younger. It looked as if Kevin, Shelly, Ben, Jason, and Elizabeth were standing in a secret garden. "Your corner of heaven on earth," Mother said each year.

The twins were double-your-pleasure choristers while the family sang "I Stand All Amazed" before they knelt in family prayer around Grandma Egan's chair. Grandma gave good prayers. She made everyone feel fine with her gentle words of gratitude to Heavenly Father for the mission of Jesus Christ. Her eyes had tears in them when she finished.

Then Dad said: "Easter began in heaven. You were there! You were there when this whole thing began. It began before the Creation, before time. Never forget that you were there!"

"I was there?"

"Where?"

"When?"

"Who else was there?"

"Was Mommy there?"

Questions came from everyone, and Dad smiled. "You all were there. Mom and I were there too. And Grandma and Grandpa Egan. Everybody was there. Heavenly Father, Jesus, and Satan were there too."

"Wow!"

"Yeah! Wow, wow!"

"It was a very important meeting to decide about our future.

You see, we were Heavenly Father's spirit children, and we were in a kind of heavenly home evening listening as we were told about Father's plan."

"What happened?" asked Elizabeth. "Tell us. Who spoke, Dad? I wish I could remember."

"Satan gave a talk," said Kevin.

"Yes, he did. He was responding to the Father's plan, under which every person would have a chance to learn, to grow, and to choose whether to be good or not. Heavenly Father knew it would be better for us that way. But it seems that Satan wanted to alter the plan and force everyone to be good. Jesus, though, wanted to do it the Father's way. Everyone voted. Some agreed with Jesus. Some went along with Satan. Things got pretty heated, I guess, because the scriptures tell us that there was a war in heaven over this.

"Well, what do you think, family?" asked Dad.

"A war in heaven makes me think of war somewhere else," said Shelly, laughing. "How about Jason and Kevin down below a few minutes ago?"

Grandma looked concerned. "Contention is of the devil. Stay out of his territory. Try not to quarrel with each other, or you might end up down below when you die. I'm about to die, and I know!" Grandma gently gave her advice and then slumped back in her chair.

Mother looked at each child knowingly.

"What does all of this have to do with Easter, Dad?" asked Ben.

"Life became a risk; having freedom of choice means that failure is possible. There had to be someone to help God's children. There had to be a Savior."

"Jesus!" cried one of the twins.

Everyone clapped at Jane's brilliance.

"Jesus loves *me*!" said Jewel, pointing her finger at her own little self.

"Atta girl!" said Kevin, clapping again. "You bet Jesus loves you! He loves all of us, I think."

"Kevin, what exactly did Jesus do for us?" asked Dad.

"Well, Jesus did at least two things for us. For one, he took our sins upon himself. He atoned for them. He did something for us that no one else could do. He made it possible for us to get back to the presence of Heavenly Father. Atonement means at-one-with."

"That's my missionary!" interrupted Mother.

"Two," continued Kevin. "Jesus was divine and had power over death. But he had a mission to perform, so instead of exercising that power he allowed himself to be crucified* and buried. Then on the third day he arose, alive and resurrected.* It was marvelous. So because of the fall of Adam and Eve, all mankind was subject to death; but because of Jesus, all mortals will live again."

"Resurrection! And that's why we have Easter," finished Jason. "Come on, mortals, now let's eat!"

"Not so fast, Son," cautioned Dad. "Living again isn't all there is to the plan of life. *How* will we live? Elizabeth, please recite the third Article of Faith for us."

" 'We believe that through the Atonement of Christ, all mankind may be saved, by obedience to the laws and ordinances of the Gospel.' "

"Good! Obedience. Ah! Now we're talking! After we die someday, we'll all live again, good and bad alike. But those who obey God's will and commandments can live together in Heavenly Father's presence. Only good people—pure and faithful —will be able to dwell with God."

"So what kind of people are we going to be?" asked Mother, hugging the new baby.

"Pure like the baby," responded Shelly. She looked around the room at these people she loved so much. Her eyes warmed, resting on Grandmother Egan. "Pure and faithful like Grandma. Oh, let's help each other get there, like we did for family home evening tonight."

Everyone clapped for her great idea.

---

*See "What the Words Mean."

Yes, Jesus loves us all.

Jesus is a special kind of shepherd.

Elder John R. Lasater spoke in April general conference* 1988 and told a moving personal experience that made him think of the Savior. It happened in Morocco. The group he was with were traveling at high speed in five of the king's limousines across the beautiful Moroccan countryside to see some ruins in a distant desert. As Elder Lasater's car topped the brow of a hill, the occupants noticed that the limousine in front of it had pulled off to the side of the road, so their car stopped too.

Elder Lasater recalled: "An old shepherd in the long, flowing robes of the Savior's day, was standing near the limousine in conversation with the driver. Nearby, I noted a small flock of sheep numbering not more than fifteen or twenty. . . . The king's vehicle had struck and injured one of the sheep belonging to the old shepherd. The driver . . . was explaining to him the law of the land. Because the king's vehicle had injured one of the sheep belonging to the old shepherd, he was now entitled to one hundred times its value. . . . However, under the same law, the injured sheep must be slain and the meat divided among the people. My interpreter hastily added, 'But the old shepherd will not accept the money. They never do.'

"Startled, I asked him why. And he added, 'Because of the love he has for each of his sheep.'

"It was then that I noticed the old shepherd reach down, lift the injured lamb in his arms, and place it in a large pouch on the front of his robe. He kept stroking its head, repeating the same word over and over again. When I asked the meaning of the word, I was informed, 'Oh, he is calling it by name. All of his sheep have a name, for he is their shepherd, and the good shepherds know each one of their sheep by name.' "

We show our love to Jesus by helping him in his mission of bringing "to pass the immortality and eternal life of man." We

---

*See "What the Words Mean."

show our love by being obedient. We read in the scriptures that he said, "If ye love me, keep my commandments" (John 14:15).

What Does This Mean to You?

It means that you owe something to Jesus.

1. You voted in heaven and chose to be a disciple of Jesus and to follow him instead of following Satan. Always remember Jesus.

2. He took your sins (and the sins of everyone else who has ever lived or ever will live) upon himself in a marvelous, unselfish act which caused such suffering in him that he bled from every pore. Imagine! Love him.

3. He had power over death, and yet he allowed himself to be crucified. He died that we might live. Keep his commandments.

With such a gift given to us, it is a good idea to live as an example of the believers in the third Article of Faith, which says, "We believe that through the Atonement of Christ, all mankind may be saved, by obedience to the laws and ordinances of the Gospel."

Scriptures to Study

Bible: Isaiah 53:11; Acts 2:38
Book of Mormon: Mosiah 15:8; 2 Nephi 10:25

4. We believe that the first principles and ordinances of the Gospel are: first, Faith in the Lord Jesus Christ; second, Repentance; third, Baptism by immersion for the remission of sins; fourth, Laying on of hands* for the gift of the Holy Ghost.

About the Fourth Article of Faith: Principles

Living by the first principles of the gospel of Jesus Christ is the sure way to a happy life.

When César was twelve years old, he met two missionaries from The Church of Jesus Christ of Latter-day Saints. They were in César's hometown in South America to teach anyone who would listen about Jesus and the wonderful principles of his gospel.

The missionaries were a long way from their own homes. César wondered how they could endure being away for two years from their families and friends, from familiar food, from activities they enjoyed, and from schools where they could quickly learn the skills they would need to support their own families some day.

---

*See "What the Words Mean."

The missionaries, or elders, as they were sometimes called, assured César that they were happy serving the Lord and helping people learn the truth. They told him that they were guided in their work by the Holy Ghost.

They told César that he too could know these things if he would pray for the Holy Ghost to witness* to him. They read to César from the Book of Mormon, Moroni 10:4, 5:

"And when ye shall receive these things, I would exhort you that ye would ask God, the Eternal Father, in the name of Christ, if these things are not true; and if ye shall ask with a sincere heart, with real intent, having faith in Christ, he will manifest the truth of it unto you, by the power of the Holy Ghost.

"And by the power of the Holy Ghost ye may know the truth of all things."

When César prayed, he knew these things were true. He wanted his family to hear the things the missionaries had taught him, so he invited them to his home. But his parents were not interested. They would not give permission for César to be baptized.

It was sad for César. He kept trying to share with his parents all that he was learning. Finally they told him that he could have nothing more to do with the missionaries and that he must not talk about these things anymore.

He remembered what the missionaries had taught about the fourth Article of Faith. He believed in Jesus, all right. But maybe he needed more knowledge and to repent*!

He hadn't done anything very wrong—but he teased his sisters unmercifully; most of the time his room was a small version of the city dump; and he was secretly very angry at his parents for not letting him be baptized.

César decided he needed to repent, to tell Heavenly Father he was sorry for a lot of things. He started praying harder. He prayed in the morning now as well as at night. He wanted an answer to his prayer. He wanted to be baptized.

---

*See "What the Words Mean."

He felt closer to Heavenly Father than ever before. He also felt close to Jesus. The missionaries had taught him to pray to Heavenly Father in the name of Jesus Christ. They had taught him that Heavenly Father and Jesus were two separate beings.

He knew God was listening to his prayers.

But he didn't get permission from his father to be baptized!

What he did feel was the instruction "Love your parents."

César began to show and say the love he felt for his mother and father. Instead of being angry at them for not letting him be baptized, he felt a kind of peace. He decided to be very helpful to his parents as well as loving.

One day the three of them were working in their vegetable garden while a little sister played nearby. Suddenly she screamed. She had been bitten by a poisonous spider!

They rushed her to the hospital, where she lay critically ill. César finally begged his parents to allow the missionaries to come and bless her. The parents were so heartbroken that they agreed. They even agreed to kneel and pray with the missionaries for guidance and comfort before the ordinance was performed.

After the prayer, the elders anointed* the sick girl with consecrated oil.* Then they laid their hands on her head, and through the power of the priesthood of God and in his name, they called down the powers of heaven to heal her.

She was healed. It was a miracle.

It was the beginning of real happiness for César, because a few days later another kind of miracle happened. César's father gave him permission to be baptized. Can you imagine how César felt?

At last he was baptized by immersion and confirmed a member of The Church of Jesus Christ of Latter-day Saints. He was given the gift of the Holy Ghost. César began to learn even more truth, because he now had the help of the Holy Ghost to know right from wrong, to be warned against danger, to recognize truth, and especially to witness that Heavenly Father and Jesus Christ lived and loved him.

---

*See "What the Words Mean."

The Holy Ghost manifests himself in a wide variety of ways. If we pay close attention, we learn to recognize the promptings of the Holy Ghost.

Once, when Joseph Smith was thinking a great deal about the subject of baptism for the dead,* he wrote that it was the "subject [that] seems to occupy my mind, and press itself upon my feelings the strongest" (*History of the Church* 5:148). This is a guideline for you as you try to learn to recognize the promptings of the Holy Ghost. You will feel your mind filled and your feelings flooded with a certain idea. Your heart and mind will be involved. The Holy Ghost will never lead you to do something that is not good. At no time will Satan lead you to do good. That is how you can tell the difference. You can read more about this in the Book of Mormon, Moroni 7:17.

What Does This Mean to You?

It means you will be better off in every way if you remember the first principles of the gospel, which are:

1. Faith in the Lord Jesus Christ.

When you have faith in the Lord Jesus Christ, you have the Lord as your friend. As you come to know Jesus you will love and admire him more. You will try to be like him.

2. Repentance.

You'll want God to forgive you so that you can start over and try to do what Jesus would do.

3. Baptism by immersion for the remission of sins.

When you have sincerely asked Heavenly Father to forgive you, he gives you another chance. Being baptized by immersion means that all of your sins have been washed away. God remembers them no more, and you can go forward in growth, more like Jesus.

4. The gift of the Holy Ghost.

---

*See "What the Words Mean."

You receive the gift of the Holy Ghost by the laying on of hands by someone with authority.* After this ordinance, you are ready to have the Holy Ghost enter into your life. He can be a comfort and a companion to those who live a pure life.

It is a good idea to live as an example of the believers in the fourth Article of Faith, which states: "We believe that the first principles and ordinances of the Gospel are: first, Faith in the Lord Jesus Christ; second, Repentance; third, Baptism by immersion for the remission of sins; fourth, Laying on of hands for the gift of the Holy Ghost."

Scriptures to Study

Bible: Hebrews 11; Mark 16:16
Book of Mormon: 3 Nephi 11:26
Doctrine and Covenants 130:23
Pearl of Great Price: Moses 6:64

---

*See "What the Words Mean."

5. We believe that a man must be called of God, by prophecy, and by the laying on of hands by those who are in authority, to preach the Gospel and administer in the ordinances thereof.

About the Fifth Article of Faith: Hands

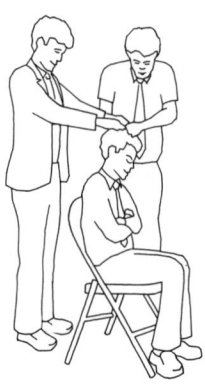

"You mean to tell me your dad is going to be a bishop?" asked Heinz in amazement.

"Yup!" Jed smiled. He was feeling good about this. It was something to have a dad who was a friend of his friends—took them fishing and all that—and who now would be the bishop of their ward too. Heinz wasn't a member of the Church, so he couldn't quite understand. Jed wanted him to know, just the same.

"Wow! Does that mean your folks are getting a divorce?"

"No. Though I guess we won't see much of Dad for awhile."

"I thought bishops weren't married. Anyway, why did he decide to be a bishop? Is he quitting his job? What will you guys do for money? Do you have to live off the collection tray offerings?"

Jed didn't realize how little Heinz knew about the way things were run in the Church. Heinz had gone with him over to the meetinghouse to play basketball in the cultural hall. He'd attended stake dances and even had taken a small part in a musical production the young people of the ward had staged. But he hadn't been to church with Jed on Sunday. Jed wondered how much he should tell his friend—and decided to explain until Heinz quit listening.

"Look, Heinz, my dad didn't just *decide* to become a bishop. He was called* by those who had power or authority to ask him. We have an Article of Faith that says, 'We believe that a man must be called of God, by prophecy, and by the laying on of hands by those who are in authority, to preach the Gospel and administer in the ordinances thereof.' "

"OK. I'm glad it's official and not just a personal whim with your dad. I like him a lot. I'd hate to see him move out away from the good times we've had with him. Will he change?" asked Heinz.

"Change? Well, he'll be busier, I guess. He'll go on working at his regular job. He'll wear his regular clothes. People will call him 'Bishop,' but he'll still be my dad and your friend. Only better. Because he'll live even closer to the Lord."

"I like that," said Heinz. "But wouldn't it be scary to be a bishop? You'd have all those icky problems to solve for people."

"Yeah, scary. From here on, for the next five years or so, I'm sure my dad will be on his knees a lot so he can get help from the Lord to help the ward members. He couldn't do it all alone, could he?"

"On his knees? I didn't know grown men really prayed. And I sure didn't know they'd pray over other people." Heinz shook his head.

"How else could Dad be a bishop—a sort of special shepherd —if he didn't pray for guidance? All those people are God's children too and my dad is responsible for them. Naturally, he'll need the power of God to help him."

---

*See "What the Words Mean."

"It's awesome!" agreed Heinz. "I guess you'll have to shape up, huh? The bishop's son. Cool."

The boys were walking to school together as they did each day. But this day was different, and both knew it. They'd been talking about holy things, but now they were silent and thoughtful as they approached the building.

Suddenly Heinz stopped and turned to his friend. "Uh, Jed . . ."

Jed stopped, too, and said a little prayer in his heart. He could see the quizzical look on Heinz's face. He really wanted his friend to understand about the blessings of the Church and be baptized. Heinz was one great kid! His only disadvantage was that he hadn't been taught the gospel.

"What?"

Heinz hesitated, then asked, "Have you ever thought about how the power of God works through a man? You say this will happen to your dad now that he is a bishop."

"Do you ever pray, Heinz?"

"Yes. A couple of years ago I lost my brother's water ski—and boy, did I pray that I could find it in that big lake before he got there for the weekend! I prayed and prayed while I rowed around that lake. And I found it!"

"You felt good about that—inside, I mean—didn't you?"

"Yeah."

"The power of God makes us feel good, tells us what to do, guides and protects us."

"How?"

Jed thought of the story he'd heard about President Harold B. Lee and finally decided to share it with Heinz. After all, he'd asked all the right questions so far. Maybe they were getting someplace with this conversion at last.

"Let me tell you a true story about Harold B. Lee, who became President of The Church of Jesus Christ of Latter-day Saints. That's the official name of the church I belong to, you know."

"I know. OK. Tell me your story."

"Well, on one occasion, years before he was the Church President, Elder Lee was in New York for a stake conference.

They were getting some new bishops and other officers that day, and after the conference Elder Lee invited the new officers and their wives to come to the setting-apart session. He placed his hands upon the new persons' heads, one by one, and through the priesthood authority he held, and in the name of Jesus Christ, he blessed the men with help from God and gave them authority to serve in God's name.

"One man was being ordained* a patriarch.*" Jed explained the calling and duties of a patriarch to his nonmember friend, then continued with his story.

"You might wonder, Heinz, how a person could do what a patriarch does. How would the power of God act through this man to reveal information about different individuals? Well afterwards the wife of the stake president told Elder Lee that an amazing thing had happened during that ordination. She suddenly felt she had to open her eyes during the sacred prayer. As she looked up at Elder Lee and the new patriarch, she saw a shaft of bright light shining on Elder Lee's head, as if it were coming through the ceiling."

"Amazing! Fantastic!" exclaimed Heinz.

"Right. Well, Elder Lee later explained that whenever faithful priesthood men lay their hands on someone's head, it is as though the Lord was putting his hands on that person. Anyway, the woman who saw this certainly knew that man was now a patriarch."

"I'm sure she did."

"Well, we'd better get in to classes. See you at lunch."

What Does This Mean to You?

It means that you belong to a church with divine authority to give you a name and a blessing, to baptize and confirm you, to bestow* the Holy Ghost upon you, to perform a lasting marriage for you some day, and to call leaders—from the ward leaders to the Presidency of the Church—to help you. And all of this is

---

*See "What the Words Mean."

acceptable before God because this is his church and these are the people he wants called at this time to help his children on earth.

Let's bring this down to the practical world to help you understand what a great blessing members of the Church have in being able to use this divine authority.

Let's say you get on a big airliner to go on a vacation. There you see young men and women dressed in that airline's official uniform. They are called flight attendants. They help the passengers in many ways. You know that what they are doing has the official sanction of that airline company because they have been trained by the company. Their uniform sets them apart from the public and tells you they are agents of that particular airline company.

Each airline has its own uniform. It keeps things orderly. Loyalties and authority are evident to the outsider or to the flying public. Remember, flight attendants couldn't just dress any way they wanted and climb aboard to start telling the passengers when to fasten their seat belts and so on. The airline wouldn't stand for it. It wouldn't be good business.

It's much more serious in a work upon which people's eternal life depends.

For church work to be accepted by God it has to be done in his church, in his way, by his power and authority.

It is a good idea to live as an example of the believers in the fifth Article of Faith, which states: "We believe that a man must be called of God, by prophecy, and by the laying on of hands by those who are in authority, to preach the Gospel and administer in the ordinances thereof."

Scriptures to Study

Bible: Exodus 3:2–10
Book of Mormon: Alma 31:36; Moroni 3:2–3
Doctrine and Covenants 42:11

6. We believe in the same organization that existed in the Primitive Church,* namely, apostles, prophets, pastors, teachers, evangelists,* and so forth.

About the Sixth Article of Faith: Organization

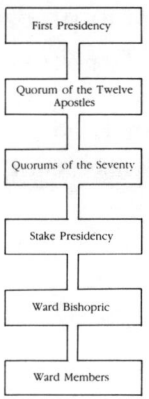

First Presidency

Quorum of the Twelve Apostles

Quorums of the Seventy

Stake Presidency

Ward Bishopric

Ward Members

Minnie was giving to the seminary class her report on the sixth Article of Faith. "Christ has always guided his children. Today in The Church of Jesus Christ of Latter-day Saints we are organized and we are taught as it was done in the primitive Church under Christ's leadership. Since the beginning, God's will and his ways have been the same for all generations of his followers," finished Minnie with a big sigh of relief.

Brother Hayes smiled and thanked Minnie. As she walked down the aisle to her seat, there was the usual rustling, stirring, and talking among class members. Some raised a hand for the "five" or mumbled compliments on her talk. *How they support each other!* Brother Hayes thought.

---

*See "What the Words Mean."

For a moment he stood silently studying the lively group of young teenagers before him. Good kids, for the most part. They got up early and came to class regularly, didn't they? Sometimes they even listened!

There were the girls with long, curly, elaborate hairstyles, wearing layers of colorful, trendy clothing and dangling earrings. There were the boys in oversized T-shirts printed with outrageous sayings, topping jeans deliberately made ragged and worn. These students didn't exactly look like disciples of Christ, but oh, what spirit they had! And how he loved them!

Brother Hayes ached to help prepare them for their important role in life. He wanted them to *know* some important things that set apart the true church of Christ on earth today from other church organizations. Brother Hayes uttered a silent prayer that he might be guided as he led a discussion about the sixth Article of Faith. It was so important.

"Okay, class, we're dividing you down the middle. You on the left are the primitive Church. You on the right are The Church of Jesus Christ of Latter-day Saints. You will answer the questions accordingly. Got it?"

"Got it!" Cliff said eagerly with his scriptures open before him.

There were a few groans, too, but a game has a way of sparking class participation, Brother Hayes knew, and once they got into it they'd like it. He said, "Primitive Church people, who was the head of the Church back in your time?"

"Jesus Christ."

"Right! And LDS people, who is head of the Church today?"

"The President of the Church?"

"Well, he's its President, but who is the head?"

Silence.

"Do you know," continued Brother Hayes, "I have heard three Presidents of the Church testify that they *knew* they were *not* the head of the Church. They knew that Jesus was at the helm, so to speak. Each said he was led and guided by Jesus to do His will on earth at this time while He is not actually living among us."

"So Jesus Christ is head of the Church today?" called out a student sitting on the right side.

"Yes. The Church is named after him, and we believe it has the same organization as the primitive Church with the same saving principles of truth taught," continued Brother Hayes. "Okay, primitive Church people, name some prophets in your day."

"Abraham, Isaac, Jacob, Noah, Moses." Out spilled the names of the familiar prophets of the Old Testament.

"LDS church people, name some of today's prophets," said Brother Hayes.

Minnie was first with "Joseph Smith."

"Joseph Smith, right! Who else?" asked Brother Hayes.

"Brigham Young. Wilford Woodruff. David O. McKay. Spencer W. Kimball. Ezra Taft Benson." The team was excited now they knew the answers.

"All right! All right! Let's talk about Apostles. People of the primitive Church, can you name any in your day? If you need help, turn to the Bible, Matthew 10:1–5."

"Is Peter one?"

"James and John the Beloved?"

"How about Judas?" The shocked class burst into response with nervous laughter.

"Sad, but true," said Brother Hayes. "Okay, today's Church people, can you name some of your Apostles?"

"Boyd K. Packer, Joseph B. Wirthlin, Dallin H. Oaks."

"Neal A. Maxwell, he's a cousin!"

"Good for you. Now let's see if we can finish the lists. You give me the names and I'll write them on the chalkboard under the correct title—primitive Church and today's true Church."

So they did.

Then Brother Hayes asked the class to open the Book of Mormon to 3 Nephi 11:21. "The organization and authority structure of the Lord's church is important, as is the way ordinances are conducted. For example, let's consider the way things were done in Christ's time on earth and note that we follow the same procedure today. Starting with Will, each take a turn reading a verse, please."

Will began, and the others followed:

"And the Lord said unto him [Nephi]: I give unto you power that ye shall baptize this people when I am again ascended into heaven.

"And again the Lord called others, and said unto them likewise; and he gave unto them power to baptize. And he said unto them: On this wise shall ye baptize; and there shall be no disputations among you.

"Verily* I say unto you, that whoso repenteth of his sins through your words, and desireth to be baptized in my name, on this wise shall ye baptize them—Behold, ye shall go down and stand in the water, and in my name shall ye baptize them.

"And now behold, these are the words which ye shall say, calling them by name, saying:

"Having authority given me of Jesus Christ, I baptize you in the name of the Father, and of the Son, and of the Holy Ghost. Amen.

"And then shall ye immerse them in the water, and come forth again out of the water.

"And after this manner shall ye baptize in my name."

"Brother Hayes, I'd like to read a scripture that has come to mean a lot to me," said Paul.

"Take it, Paul, and give us the reference, please."

"It's from the Doctrine and Covenants, 76:50–53:

"And again we bear record—for we saw and heard, and this is the testimony of the gospel of Christ concerning them who shall come forth in the resurrection of the just—

"They are they who received the testimony of Jesus, and believed on his name and were baptized after the manner of his burial, being *buried* in the water in his name, and this according to the commandment which he has given—

"That by keeping the commandments they might be washed and cleansed from all their sins."

---

*See "What the Words Mean."

"You see," added Paul. "Sprinkling just doesn't do it, does it? That's how I was baptized when I was a baby—into another church, of course—with sprinkling! And with sprinkling, when you know what you're doing you surely don't get the same picture of starting life over, as you do with being buried in the water and coming forth clean."

The discussion in that seminary class reminds us of the consistency in Christ's church, whether in early times or today in The Church of Jesus Christ of Latter-day Saints.

Following Christ's crucifixion and the subsequent deaths of his Apostles,* the church he had organized began to change. It didn't take long for people to begin to worship according to their own ways and not according to God's plan or instruction. By the time Joseph Smith prayed in the grove to ask which church was true, a restoration of the gospel and the God-given church organization was needed.

Today, with truth restored, we find the following evidence that this is the Lord's church:

1. The name of his church is as Christ dictated it.

2. The same organization exists in the Church today as in the primitive Church.

3. The Church has the fullness of the gospel as taught by Christ.

4. Every ordinance* and doctrine in The Church of Jesus Christ of Latter-day Saints has been revealed by God.

What Does This Mean to You?

It means that you can be grateful you belong to the Church of Jesus Christ and that you should seek to spread this blessing by sharing the gospel with others whenever you can.

It means that the Church you belong to has the organization and authority to preserve truth, to protect against error in information and procedures.

---

*See "What the Words Mean."

It means that leaders who help you grow up are indeed called of God. They will try to perform according to his will. This will make a difference in how you feel about going to church, studying the gospel, and trying to become more like Jesus.

It means that as you move through life you can solve problems according to God's plan and principles.

It is a good idea to live as an example of the believers in the sixth Article of Faith, which says, "We believe in the same organization that existed in the Primitive Church, namely, apostles, prophets, pastors, teachers, evangelists, and so forth."

Scriptures to Study

Bible: John 15:16; Acts 6:1–6; Ephesians 4:11–14
Book of Mormon: Mosiah 23:17; 3 Nephi 12:1
Doctrine and Covenants 41:11

7.   We believe in the gift of tongues, prophecy, revelation,*
visions, healing, interpretation of tongues, and so forth.

About the Seventh Article of Faith: Gifts

Everyone loves to get a gift. But when the gift comes from
God, it is wonderful!

The seventh Article of Faith is all about gifts. First we are given
the gift of the Holy Ghost. Then if we live in obedience, we can
be blessed with certain spiritual gifts* of the Holy Ghost, such as
the gift of tongues,* revelations that change lives for the better,
and healing blessings.

Belonging to the Church of Jesus Christ and learning to be a
true believer strengthens your faith and puts you in a position to
receive gifts of the Spirit, gifts that make you a better person, a
happier person, and a more effective helper in the kingdom of
God on earth.

It is like what happened to Briton. His grandmother gave him a
big, fluffy comforter for his birthday. It was great. He could curl

---

*See ''What the Words Mean.''

53

up in it on cold nights to read. He could stretch out on it to watch television. He could take it to a cousin's house for a sleep-over. He could flop it over himself when he knelt down by his bed to pray in the winter months.

And he could make his bed in a second!

Having that comforter about him warmed his heart, too. It made him feel secure. And so do the Holy Ghost and the spiritual gifts a person can enjoy if he or she keeps faithful.

Mary Wilson tells a story about her grandmother, Zina Diantha Huntington Young.

When Zina was a young girl about your age, she was given the gift of speaking in tongues.*

One Sunday, Zina stood up in fast* meeting to bear her testimony. Suddenly the Holy Spirit filled her and surrounded her. Her heart began to beat hard and fast. Her eyes watered. The palms of her hands felt damp. Then an amazing thing happened. Zina began speaking in tongues.

Everyone, including Zina, was startled. Some little children in the congregation were not in tune and didn't realize that this was a very sacred moment. They began to giggle a bit because Zina had changed languages. And they could not understand her.

Even the grown-ups whispered to each other. Surely something unusual was happening. Many of them wept. They stared at Zina.

Zina felt very self-conscious and not herself.

Zina did not ever want to have that happen again because she did not know what to do about it.

Zina asked her mother about this experience.

Sister Hungtington said that it was the gift of the Holy Ghost and that it came to Zina because the Lord loved her and had a special way of showing it.

Well, Zina didn't want to have this spiritual gift because it made her different from the other children. She promised herself

---

*See "What the Words Mean."

that if ever that feeling came over her again, she would pay no attention to it. She certainly wouldn't stand and speak in a strange language, even if it was the language of God!

Her mother tried to comfort her. She explained that this was a problem that Zina would have to settle with God. Sister Huntington might have read to Zina from the Book of Mormon, Jacob 6:8, which says: "Will ye . . . deny . . . the power of God, and the gift of the Holy Ghost, and quench the Holy Spirit?"

Since the beginning of time people who have special missions to perform on earth have wrestled with God on the things he has wanted them to do. We each have to grow in spirituality and in knowledge of how God works and why.

Zina wrestled too. She loved Heavenly Father. She loved Jesus. She wanted to do what was right. She finally decided to go to Heavenly Father and confess her feelings. She would find a quiet place where she wouldn't be bothered and she would earnestly pray for Heavenly Father to help her.

Bright sunshine, fragrant meadow grasses, and flowers wrapped around Zina as she made her lonely but determined walk to the far corner of the family property. She found her private place behind thick bushes growing beneath the poplar trees. There Zina knelt in prayer.

She called upon Heavenly Father in the name of Jesus Christ as she had been taught to do every time she prayed since she was a little girl. She explained her problem.

A sacred, amazing feeling enveloped Zina like a warm comforter or blanket. Zina understood with her heart and her mind that her prayers had been heard. She had a response from God.

First, she knew that if she did not accept the spiritual gift from God, if she did not use it, it would be taken away from her altogether! She would be estranged from Jesus.

Second, she knew that if she put her trust in God she wouldn't feel awkward. She could stand for the Lord among her friends. And she knew that being young or being an adult had nothing to do with when and how God bestowed his spiritual gifts.

This was important and real to Zina. She quickly repented. She promised Heavenly Father that she would be grateful and obedient instead of embarrassed or selfish. She would accept the sacred spiritual gift. No matter if silly children giggled because they didn't understand!

Zina accepted her spiritual gifts all along the path of her life. She grew up to be a wife of Brigham Young and a great spiritual strength to the sisters in Relief Society throughout all the Church.

God never does anything that isn't for the good of his children. You can read about this in section 46 of the Doctrine and Covenants. These gifts follow the believer, the person of faith. They are given for the benefit of those who love the Lord and keep his commandments—or who earnestly strive to do so.

Every faithful Church member is given a gift by the Spirit of God. We don't all receive every gift.

It would be confusing if everyone had the gift of prophecy for everyone else.

It would be limiting if only a few had the gift of teaching and testifying of the gospel of Jesus Christ.

Some of us will receive the gift to know by the Holy Ghost that Jesus is truly the Son of God.

Some will believe on the words of others that Jesus is the Christ.

Some will be given the faith to heal and be healed.

Some will speak in tongues on occasion.

What Does This Mean to You?

It means that you would do well to do more than memorize the seventh Article of Faith. You'll want to apply it to your life. Maybe you'll need to be healed. Maybe you'll want to fill the particular purpose for which you came to earth, and to do this you will need vision for your life, strength to avoid temptation, direction to prepare for service in the kingdom of God on earth, and a fulfillment of your desire for a testimony of Jesus.

Here is a scripture especially for you: "Let no man despise thy youth; but *be thou an example of the believers,* in word, in conversation, in charity, in spirit, in faith, in purity. . . . Neglect not the gift that is in you." (1 Timothy 4:12, 14; italics added.)

OK. Now, that means:

No dirty talk.

No joking about sacred Church things.

No disrespect for parents or others in authority over you.

No self-pity, no selfishness.

No contention or quarreling.

No immoral behavior or thoughts.

It means doing what you know to be right and true and good for you, no matter who giggles, coaxes, forces, or teases you! You are *you,* and you are precious and important and loved by God.

It is a good idea to live as an example of the believers in the seventh Article of Faith, which says, "We believe in the gift of tongues, prophecy, revelation, visions, healing, interpretation of tongues, and so forth."

Scriptures to Study

Bible: Mark 16:17, 18; Luke 10:17
Book of Mormon: Alma 9:21
Doctrine and Covenants 46:11

8. We believe the Bible to be the word of God as far as it is translated correctly; we also believe the Book of Mormon to be the word of God.

About the Eighth Article of Faith: Scriptures

How would you like to go to sleep at night with two ancient Egyptian mummies* beneath your bed?

In the discussion of the seventh Article of Faith, we told a story about a remarkable young woman who grew up to be an amazing adult. It was she who had to sleep over the mummies! Her name was Zina Diantha Huntington Young.

Hearing stories about others can excite us into trying to be like them.

For example, here is another incident from the life of Zina. Zina's father, William Huntington, a well-to-do farmer, was not happy with the church that the family attended. He decided to study the Bible and learn about the primitive Church, the one in the Savior's day. Then he and his family would join the church that was the most similar to the one Christ organized during his mortal ministry (see the discussion of the sixth Article of Faith). William discovered, however, that none of the churches had the same organization or doctrines as the early Church. There were no prophets or Apostles. There were no demonstrations of spiritual gifts (see the discussion of the seventh Article of Faith). It was very

---

*See ''What the Words Mean.''

disappointing to Mr. Huntington that he couldn't find such a church.

Now, as Latter-day Saints we know that in spite of the many churches in the world, and their many devoted ministers, preachers, and members, an apostasy* had occurred on earth, a falling-away from the truth. It began after Jesus was crucified and his Apostles had died. This apostasy is the reason why the truth and fullness of the gospel had to be restored, as it finally was through Joseph Smith.

Zina's father prayed to God that he might be shown the true Church. Not long afterward, he heard stories about a new prophet who possessed a "new, golden Bible." Mr. Huntington was anxious to meet this prophet and to see his "Bible." One day Hyrum Smith, a brother to Joseph, and David Whitmer, one of the three witnesses* of the Book of Mormon, were doing missionary work in the area where the Huntington family lived. They knocked on the door at the Huntington home. Mr. Huntington felt these men were an answer to his prayer, and he invited them in.

These missionaries taught Mr. Huntington the gospel and left him a copy of the Book of Mormon, or the "golden Bible," as people called it because it had been translated from gold plates.

When Zina came home from school, almost the first thing she saw as she came into the house was the "gold Bible." She was drawn to it like a magnet and read with wonder the words on the cover, *The Book of Mormon.* Immediately the Spirit whispered within her that this book was the word of God. She picked it up and clasped it to her, crying, "This is the truth, truth, truth!"

Soon everyone in Zina's family, except one brother, was baptized. They were anxious to be with the main group of the Church, and so they soon moved to Kirtland, Ohio, to join the Saints there.

They became very helpful in building up the Church, which was patterned after the Church of Christ's day that Mr. Huntington had wanted to find for so long. In fact, the Huntington family was so helpful that they even agreed to take four ancient Egyptian

---

*See "What the Words Mean."

mummies and hide them so that the enemies of the new church couldn't destroy them. These mummies, you see, concealed the precious papyri* from which the book of Abraham was translated.

Now you know why these strange but valuable relics were hidden under Zina's bed!

Marion G. Romney was a brilliant scholar of the scriptures, a delightful humorist, a deeply spiritual man, and a successful attorney. But most important, perhaps, were the facts that he was a loving father and that he was a counselor to President Spencer W. Kimball in the First Presidency of the Church.

There is a tender story you should know about President Romney as you try to be better at scripture study. Brother Romney used to enjoy reading the scriptures out loud with his son. One night they were in the son's bedroom, with the boy on the top bunk bed and Brother Romney on the lower bunk. Each would take a turn reading certain verses from the Book of Mormon.

Brother Romney had often borne his testimony of his love for the Book of Mormon and of the witness he had through the Holy Ghost that it was a true translation from ancient records of disciples of the Savior. This particular night there was an especially good spirit as father and son shared the truths from that book. When the younger Romney had finished taking a turn, he said solemnly, "Dad, just a minute, I'd like to ask you something. Have you ever felt like crying when you read the Book of Mormon?"

"Yes, son, indeed I have."

"Well, I'm crying now," replied the boy, almost whispering as his voice broke with emotion.

Brother Romney felt the tears push against his own eyelids. Imagine! His young son was feeling the powerful witness through the Holy Ghost that the Book of Mormon was true.

President Romney said later, "I feel certain that if, in our homes, parents will read from the Book of Mormon prayerfully

---

*See "What the Words Mean."

and regularly, both by themselves and with their children, the spirit of that great book will come to permeate our homes and all who dwell therein. The spirit of reverence will increase; mutual respect and consideration for each other will grow. The spirit of contention will depart. Parents will counsel their children in greater love and wisdom. Children will be more responsive and submissive to the counsel of their parents. Righteousness will increase. Faith, hope, and charity—the pure love of Christ—will abound in our homes and lives, bringing in their wake peace, joy, and happiness." (Marion G. Romney, in Conference Report, April 1960, pp. 110–13).

Such a thing can happen to you, too. You can know that the Book of Mormon is true if you read it and get down on your knees in some private place and ask Heavenly Father, in the name of Jesus Christ, if this book is true.

For example, did those ancient Nephites really live on the American continent?

Did they baptize by immersion?

Did they have sacramental prayers as we know them?

Without television or telephone, how did they know when Christ was crucified and resurrected in another part of the world, across the land and the waters?

Were they taught truths by Jesus Christ himself?

Yes! But find out for yourself.

We say we believe the Book of Mormon to be true and the Bible to be true as far as it is translated correctly. This is because those who kept the records included in the Book of Mormon did so by command and guidance of God—right down to Moroni, the last recorder.

In one place in the Book of Mormon it reads: "Behold I, Moroni, do finish the record of my father, Mormon. Behold, I have but few things to write, which things I have been commanded by my father. . . . Therefore I will write and hide up the records in the earth; and whither I go it mattereth not." (Mormon 8:1, 4.) Then Moroni explained that he couldn't write much because he didn't have room upon the plates and he had no ore to make additional plates. He couldn't get ore because he was all alone. All his friends and family, as well as his father, had been slain by the enemy.

Moroni finished his account. Then he hid up the plates.

These are the "gold plates" that Joseph Smith found hundreds of years later with the help of Moroni, who was now a resurrected being and an angel.

Joseph Smith kept very close to the Lord as he grew through his teenage years. At last he was ready and able to translate from the plates with the help of the Urim and Thummim* and through the power of the Holy Ghost.

Now, as to the Bible. During the early stages of the apostasy we spoke of above, wicked men deliberately took away from the Bible records many "plain and precious parts" (see 1 Nephi 13:26–27). So the Bible, great and powerful as it is, has not come down to us today in its original and proper form. In addition, for centuries copies had to be made by hand and this introduced errors and problems for modern translators.

Emil G. Kraeling, a scholar of Bible history, has this to say: "When the Hebrew Old Testament causes us difficulty on some particular point, and when we are convinced that its wording has been damaged in some way . . . we must remember that in copying texts by hand a thoughtless person could leave out words, miswrite words, jump to the wrong line, or misread the older manuscript. Furthermore, passages may have writing that was illegible or gaps caused by damage from worms or rodents or crumbling from age." (Emil G. Kraeling, *Rand McNally Bible Atlas,* p. 20.)

You can understand that. Sometimes you copy things out of books or rewrite things other people have prepared. It is easy to make mistakes as you do your homework by hand. But if the pages were many hundreds of years old, if they were in an unfamiliar language, and if you didn't know much about the traditions and customs of that other place and time in history, truth could get distorted.

---

*See "What the Words Mean."

This happened to some extent in the case of the Bible because of the way in which it has come to us. That way is very different from the way in which the Book of Mormon was brought forth and translated. This is why we say that we believe the Bible to be the word of God "as far as it is translated correctly." But we must remember that the Bible is a precious and sacred book, one we should read often and come to love and enjoy.

What Does This Mean to You?

The Bible has many important things to help us in our lives. There are stories of the relationship of God to his children on earth. There are the Ten Commandments; the beautiful Psalms; and the prophecies of Isaiah and other prophets, including some prophecies that have come to pass, proving that the prophets were in tune with God.

It means that you and I can have the word of God as it has been given to his children since earliest times on earth. Let's remember how blessed we are, as members of the Church, to have the perfect translation of the Book of Mormon. It is up to us to help bring the book to others who don't know of this great blessing.

It means that God still loves his children, each generation, as they come to earth to learn and grow. As he had in ancient times, he has wisdom to help us in these times. There is more truth, truth that is just right for us now, that is being revealed to God's prophets in our day.

It is a good idea to live as an example of the believers in the eighth Article of Faith, which says, "We believe the Bible to be the word of God as far as it is translated correctly; we also believe the Book of Mormon to be the word of God."

Scriptures to Study

Bible: Isaiah 29:4; Ezekiel 37:15–20
Book of Mormon: 1 Nephi 13:26
Doctrine and Covenants 42:12

9. We believe all that God has revealed, all that He does now reveal, and we believe that He will yet reveal many great and important things pertaining to the Kingdom of God.

About the Ninth Article of Faith: Revelation

Consider this story about a boy named Andrew and his friends Eric and Sam. It is just a story, of course, but it stirs up possibilities that make your heart flutter.

Andrew slammed the screen door as he pitched through it to the lawn beyond. He leaped over his two friends, already snuggled in their sleeping bags, and slammed into his own.

"Did you bring anything to eat?" asked Eric.

"Is that all you think about, Eric?" Andrew laughed and tossed bags of Twizzlers and M&Ms to his friends.

"Yes," replied Eric, snatching the treats.

"Well, think about this. Do you believe there are people up there on the stars?"

"Do *you* believe it, Andrew? If you believe it, I'll believe it," said Eric lightly. Then he swallowed a wad of licorice. "Say, did

you bring out anything to drink?'' He was quick to catch the can
of soda that Andrew airmailed to him.

''Come on, Andrew, people on stars?''

''Yes, people. Like us. I'm not talking E.T. or weirdo types
from Star Trek stories.''

''Eric's a weirdo type,'' said Sam, making a bull's-eye shot
with an M&M to Eric's head.

''Be serious, guys. I have a reason. Look up there, straight
overhead. Can you see the Big Dipper?''

''Wow! That's a grundle of stars. How am I supposed to find
the Big Dipper?''

Andrew pointed out the bright North Star and described the
crooked handle and square-shaped scoop of the familiar
constellation. ''Got it, Sam?''

''Got it.''

''Got it, Eric?''

''Sure, I know about the Big Dipper. I'm a Boy Scout boy,
remember?''

''Good. Now, what about people up there—you know,
people like us?''

''Well, if there are people like us up there, heaven help 'em,''
chortled Sam through the licorice.

''Listen, you guys are my friends. I just have to tell you
something. Promise not to tell?''

And the duet's ''Yeah! Yeah!'' moved Andrew forward with
his story.

''Just now when I went in for the supplies, I overheard my
parents talking in their bedroom. I was going to ask Mom where
the popcorn was, but Dad sounded kind of different as he talked,
so I stopped and listened outside their door.''

''So what does that parent stuff have to do with us?''

''It was about the Big Dipper and Dad's space computer.''

''Oh yeah?''

''Yes, NASA stuff. You know he's in charge of the control
room's master computer that tracks spaceships and all that.''

''Sure, we know your dad is a big deal. Lead on, Skywalker.
Beam me up,'' drawled Sam.

Slowly Andrew told what he had overheard. While his father was tracking a missile, the computer picture had been interrupted by "ghosting." His dad had seen the missile on one side of the monitor, and on the other side appeared the image of a man—not a Pac Man but a real man. Andrew's dad looked over all the controls and connections, including the laser converter. Everything checked out. It could only mean that the interference was from outside the control center, not part of the missile connection.

"That's it, guys. What do you think?" finished Andrew.

"I think maybe your house is haunted," said Eric.

"I think maybe I should go home," said Sam, piling out of his sleeping bag.

"It isn't the *house* that's haunted, Licorice Legs!" exploded Andrew. "It's the computer! So stay put, because we have to talk."

"Right! I'll talk to you, but I am not talking to any spook from outer space."

Sam sat on top of his sleeping bag, crossed his legs, and said: "All right, listen to me. These are the facts: One: There's been a message from space. That means there are people up there. Two: This is the most excitement we've had around this neighborhood since I was born. I think it would be fun to see if we could make the space connection. Three: Time's a-wasting. I say we hit your dad's computer and hit it *now*!"

"You call that fun—getting ourselves arrested or worse for fooling around with space center computers? Hey, guys, this is me leaving," announced Eric, making a mess of his sleeping bag as he rose to his feet and sprinted toward the street.

Andrew was after him in a flash to bring him back. "You can't go now. You know the secret. We're in this together. Besides, if you leave here raving about this, Dad could lose his job or something. You just can't go now." Andrew held his grip on Eric's arm until the boy settled down again. "OK, go on, Sam. Do you have any ideas?"

There was long silence, but then Sam said, "Yes. I have a feeling there is something that we need to do about this. Wake up your dad, Andrew, and offer our services."

"Wake up my dad?" echoed Andrew.

"He'd kill us!" wailed Eric. "Andrew, you know he'd thump us all. First, you listen to something you are not supposed to hear. Then you spread the news. Now you want to wake him up from a sound sleep and tell an angry dad that we're here to help!"

"Good thinking, Eric. You know my dad."

Sam was not giving up. "Dads are all alike. So I say we work without your dad."

"How?" Then Andrew answered his own question. "Maybe we could just break into Dad's personal computer room here at home. It's hooked into the mainframe at the center. Dad has taught me about computers in his studio here, and I think I can find the access code. Maybe we could make that Big Dipper middle star connection."

"Maybe we could all go jump in the lake with computers tied to our feet," jeered Eric.

"Silence, worm," insisted Sam. "Andrew, why do we have to break in when it's your home?"

"Because the only way to Dad's studio inside the house is through my parents' bedroom, and they're sleeping there. We'd wake them up for sure. We'll have to break in from the outside."

As if on command, the boys raced to the studio door. It was, of course, locked tight, as were the windows. But there was hope. There was a "puppy door" close to the ground, a door which was used by delivery men who deposited top secret tapes and reels. Someone would have to wiggle through that. The three husky boys looked each other over. Eric dropped to his knees by the trap door and began barking like a puppy.

"Shhhh!" Andrew made his hand a muzzle over Eric's mouth.

Sam put his foot on Eric's bottom and tried to nudge him through the small door. "Get Katie, Andrew. We're too big."

Katie was one agile little dancer. While the boys held up the puppy door flap and pushed and poked at Katie, she managed to squirm her way through. For a little sister she was OK.

"All *right*!" they chorused.

Now if she would just open the door! Andrew whispered instructions one more time to the sleepy little girl, and suddenly the deadbolt turned from its channel and the door was open.

"We're in!"

"We're dead!" moaned Eric, throwing himself on the ground.

"We are if you don't keep still."

Andrew turned on the studio lights and sat in front of his father's computer. Quietly, carefully, he went to work.

He dialed the control center.

He responded to the computer queries on the terminal by entering the correct password and ID.

When they were hooked in by modem, he repeatedly punched in the commands, while he mouthed the words, "Come in, Ursa Major. Come in, middle star. Come in, Big Dipper."

Eric whispered to Andrew, "Do you think you can beat this system?"

"I dunno. I just thought I'd send a message and wait. They'll have to contact us as they did Dad," replied Andrew.

They didn't have long to wait. It was as if the messenger on the middle star had been standing by for generations of light years just to reach these particular young men at this particular time on earth. "Hello, Earth. Hello, Earth youth. We have a message especially for youth who will usher in the twenty-first century."

Eric nudged Sam, who nudged Andrew, who squeezed Katie, who shivered. She hadn't left his side.

The startled boys gaped at the transmissions on the computer screen. Their hearts pounded and their mouths felt dry. They also felt important. And frightened.

"Andrew, look at that! Their lips are moving. Can you pull up the audio?"

"I'll try." In moments, sound came through just as the man said, "I am Philo T. Farnsworth."

"Philo Farnsworth!" exclaimed Andrew. "Great shooting stars! That man has been dead for ages. He was my grandmother's relative. He sort of invented television. My mother reminds me of this every time I turn on the TV."

"Well, he's acting real alive now."

"Shh!" Sam was anxious to hear the message.

"And let me introduce my friends: Amelia Earhart, Ben Franklin, Madam Curie, Galileo, Christopher Columbus, Babe Ruth, and Brigham Young. We're here on middle star temporarily, discussing the problems facing this generation of youth. Please, carefully listen to Florence Nightingale."

The woman's kindly face appeared, and she said, "Youth, pray! I was sixteen when I prayed to God for direction in my life. He spoke to me. I was called to establish proper nursing schools and improved medical care. Oh, many lives were saved down the years. For this work I was the first woman to receive Britain's Order of Merit. Now, youth, what can *you* do for others in *your* world? My counsel to you is to pray. Pray for guidance to see what only you can do."

Her image was replaced by Thomas Edison's, and he said, "Youth ushering in the twenty-first century, prepare! Prepare to contribute in your own special way. Don't waste your lives. I was just your age when I lived on earth in 1857. I didn't go to a school like yours. My mother was my tutor. She gave me a primer on physics which described certain experiments that I could do myself. Then one day I started experimenting with electricity. After that I invented many things for mankind, including the light bulb, the phonograph, and more. I received a special congressional gold medal for my work. Youth, prepare yourselves to make a difference!"

Philo spoke again. "I was born in Earth year 1906 on a farm in Idaho. I was fourteen before I even knew such a thing as electricity existed. But then through prayer, through preparation of my skills and mind, and through my experimenting, too, I was able to grasp the principles that produced an electronic television system suitable for homes. Earth youth in these last days, be guided by God in your lives. Be guided by God. Pray . . . prepare . . . perform! Earth's future depends upon you.''

Silence.

To the young viewers it was awesome.

The boys didn't say a word as they watched the patterns of light and dark snake across the screen as the figures disappeared.

Andrew shut off the computer and turned off the room light. Carrying sleepy Katie, he ushered his friends out of the door.

Nobody spoke until they were safe in their sleeping bags, including Katie, whom Andrew stuffed into his. He couldn't have her waking up their parents and spilling their adventure.

"Hey! Was that a dream or what?" Sam asked finally.

"We're talking about nightmares . . . those people want us to work!" Eric said, groaning.

"That's not all bad if you're doing interesting stuff."

"That Big Dipper up there will never seem the same to me," said Eric.

"Nor will life," added Andrew.

This is just a story, but it makes you think, doesn't it? What if . . . ?

Well, more marvelous things than that have happened. Since the beginning of time, God has told his children on earth important things.

He revealed to Joseph Smith the translation of the metal plates hidden up by Moroni.

He revealed to Brigham Young that the Great Salt Lake Valley was the place where the Saints should settle.

He revealed to President Spencer W. Kimball that it was time for worthy men of all races to be given the priesthood.

He has revealed sacred words, prayers, and methods for the ordinances of sacrament, baptism, and temple work.

He revealed the Word of Wisdom. Joseph Smith told the Church members about the harm in tobacco and alcohol and other substances, more than 150 years ago. Now science is catching up and proving that the Word of Wisdom is true!

God has many ways of giving revelation regarding the kingdom of God.

The important thing is to remember that we believe that God does reveal truth to us—he always has and always will. We also believe what he reveals.

What Does This Mean to You?

It means that continual revelation is a special blessing. With it, we not only know more about the workings of earthly things; we are also in a position to receive knowledge about spiritual things. There is still so much to learn.

We know that we are alive, but we know little about how death works.

We know that Christ lives, but we know nothing about how resurrection happens.

We marvel at the miracle of babies, but we know nothing about when the spirit sent from heaven enters the body of the infant.

There is more. Live to learn about it.

It is a good idea to live as an example of the believers in the ninth Article of Faith: "We believe all that God has revealed, all that He does now reveal, and we believe that He will yet reveal many great and important things pertaining to the Kingdom of God."

Scriptures to Study

Bible: Joel 2:28; John 5:39
Book of Mormon: Mormon 8:16; 1 Nephi 13:26

10. We believe in the literal gathering of Israel and in the restoration of the Ten Tribes; that Zion (the New Jerusalem) will be built upon the American continent; that Christ will reign personally upon the earth; and, that the earth will be renewed and receive its paradisiacal glory.

About the Tenth Article of Faith: Gathering

The tenth Article of Faith is about getting our Heavenly Father's family together for a colossal family reunion. And it is about the Millennium,* when Christ will come to earth to reign.

There are four parts to the tenth Article of Faith. You'll want to understand each part. The parts contain very exciting ideas. We believe these things and know that they are important to us.

1. The literal* gathering of Israel* and the restoration of the ten tribes.*
2. Zion* (the New Jerusalem*) will be built upon the American continent.
3. Christ will reign personally upon the earth.
4. The earth will receive its paradisiacal* glory.*

We will consider these four points of the tenth Article of Faith one at a time to help you understand what it is you believe in and

*See "What the Words Mean."

what it means to you. The tenth Article of Faith is a very important one because it has to do with the final scenes of this earth and the glorious period of the Millennium.

The Literal Gathering. In each generation of time God has had a group of his children who were especially important to his work, which is to bring to pass the immortality and eternal life of all of his family. You are a member of that important group today.

In ancient times father Abraham and his posterity had this responsibility.

Hundreds of millions of people have been Israelites, heirs to the blessings and covenants* made with their ancestors—blessings they will receive if they are worthy. Ten of those tribes became scattered because they resisted God's will.

The literal gathering of Israel is about bringing those worthy ones back into the fold of God.

This is going on today through missionary and temple work. People across the world are being taught the gospel.

A patriarchal blessing* will tell you your lineage*—that means it will tell you which of the tribes of Israel you stem from.

The New Jerusalem. When Christ comes to reign personally on earth and to usher in the Millennium, the world's familiar governments will be changed. There will be government under God, and there will be two world capitals. One will be Jerusalem in the Holy Land on Zion's hill, known as such since King David's day generations ago. The other will be the New Jerusalem to be built in Jackson County, Missouri. It will also be known as the City of Zion.

There are many prophecies and references to these two great centers of government during the Millennium. The law and the word of God will go forth from them. You can read about this in Isaiah 2:3, which says, "For out of Zion shall go forth the law, and the word of the Lord from Jerusalem."

---

*See "What the Words Mean."

Christ Will Reign. When Christ comes again to earth, it will be to bring peace. The scriptures tell us that he will come at the height of the world's wars and wickedness. But he will be known, at last, by *all* the people on earth. Peace will come and will last a thousand years. The wicked will not stand. Satan will not have power to tempt people until after the thousand years.

The Renewal and Glory of Earth. You probably know that the word *century* means one hundred years. Did you know that *millennium* means one thousand years? That may seem a long time, because most people on earth today live an average of seventy years or so.

The earth will be renewed when Christ comes to reign. It will be returned to its paradisiacal state, which means it will be as it was when the creation of earth was completed and Adam and Eve were placed in the Garden of Eden. God declared then that all he had done was "very good." You can read about this in your Bible, in Genesis 1:31.

What Does This Mean to You?

It means that you will want to watch your own actions and choices. You will want to watch the details of your own life so that you will be found worthy to be in on the great gathering at the time of Christ's second coming.*

It means that since you are of the house of Israel, you'll want to be at the "family reunion" when the lost tribes (scattered because of sin and withdrawal) are literally gathered together again.

It means that you have new understanding about God's love for his children. At first glance life may seem especially hard for some people on earth. But you know that God loves all of his children. It's just that not all of God's children love him!

---

*See "What the Words Mean."

Meanwhile, it is a good idea to live as an example of the believers in the tenth Article of Faith: "We believe in the literal gathering of Israel and in the restoration of the Ten Tribes; that Zion (the New Jerusalem) will be built upon the American continent; that Christ will reign personally upon the earth; and, that the earth will be renewed and receive its paradisiacal glory."

Scriptures to Study

Bible: Deuteronomy 30:1–3; Matthew 24:31
Book of Mormon: Ether 13:6
Pearl of Great Price: Moses 7:62

11. We claim the privilege* of worshiping Almighty God according to the dictates* of our own conscience, and allow all men the same privilege, let them worship how, where, or what they may.

About the Eleventh Article of Faith: Worship

Let's pretend that you are a tourist in Jerusalem. You have gone with your tour group to visit the Dome of the Rock. There are many traditions about the rock. Some say it is the place where Mohammed ascended to heaven. Others say it is on the site of Solomon's temple. Some guides describe the rock as the place where Abraham took his son Isaac to offer him as a sacrifice.

Whatever the guides tell you or whatever people believe, it is considered sacred ground by all. There is an exquisite church or mosque built over the huge rock to protect it. People come from many lands to worship there.

As you stand outside watching the visitors—these pilgrims*—you notice something besides the strange languages that are

---

*See "What the Words Mean."

spoken or the colors of their skin or their styles of clothing. You notice how they prepare to worship.

Most are not self-conscious about what they do. They are not aware, or they do not notice, that they are different from others in their style of worship. It is as if they are the only people in the world in that place. They are intent on paying homage to their God in the way they have been taught.

On the grounds about the dome there are fountains and pools, troughs with running water, niches to store sandals, basins on pedestals, prayer rugs, pews, and certain religious symbols such as the crucifix.

Before the worshipers enter the church, some busily remove their sandals and wash their feet in a trough. Some remove their shoes and put them together in a niche. Some dip their fingers in the basin of holy water and touch their forehead, chest, and shoulders in the sign of the cross. Some carry sacred beads. Some pause by a pool and wrap their heads in turbans. Some remove their hats or caps. Some tie on a kind of apron. Some unfold their prayer rug and drape it over one shoulder before going inside. Some keep bowing and nodding all the way from the fountain area to the inner sanctum. Some light candles as they say a special prayer.

As a Latter-day Saint you would do none of those things. But you would do other things; you would remove your shoes if you went inside a holy temple and you would wear special white clothing to do the work there. You wore white clothing when you were baptized too. And you were immersed in water.

Sometimes along the River Jordan outside of Jerusalem, near the spot where, according to tradition, Jesus was baptized, there will be groups conducting their own baptismal ceremonies. Once when I visited the Holy Land, I saw a large group of people dressed in black clothing. The baptism was done by immersion. Then, as the person was brought up out of the water, everyone on shore would chorus, "Hallelujah!"

That might be surprising to you, but to them it was an appropriate and moving religious experience.

It is fascinating to watch the wide variety in worship.

If you were to go to Bangkok, you would visit an elaborate, colorful, exotic building behind a wall. It sparkles. It was featured in the movie *The King and I*, starring Yul Brynner and Deborah Kerr. It has many ledges and small walls where the worshipers curl up or kneel and stay for long hours in sacred meditation. This building is very sacred to the people.

In China you would see great, dark shrines filled with smoke from incense and candles. The air is oppressive. Today, you wouldn't see many who actually are there to worship. Only tourists move in and out of the shrines, because Communism has made ancient traditions of worship unfashionable.

In Kyoto, Japan, you would visit the shrine of a thousand Buddhas. For some people, that is the ultimate place to worship. Since Buddha is a kind of deity* to some Japanese, to be surrounded by a thousand Buddhas is a joyful experience, particularly for old people preparing to die.

Wherever a devoted Muslim is, there is his prayer rug. His discipline of prayers offered out loud at certain times of the day is strictly kept. Once a fine-looking gentleman in a Western-style suit slipped a turban on his head and spread his prayer rug on the sidewalk in front of the Hotel Utah in downtown Salt Lake City. He knelt down, faced the east, and began his sacred chant. It was that time of day for him, and he seemed unaware of the startled people passing by.

In the far corners of the Philippine islands you'd worship with a family in a grass hut. There would be a simple Christian hymn, a prayer read from a book, and then the young people who can read would share some scripture from the Bible.

Every person on earth is a child of God, spiritually created by him. These spirit children were sent from God's presence to dwell in a physical body prepared by earthly parents. A veil of forgetfulness is drawn over the mind, closing out the memory of our premortal life. This is done so that learning and growing and testing can happen.

People may worship in ways that differ little or a lot from

---

*See "What the Words Mean."

others. The important thing is that there are good people across the world who seek solace and direction from the only God they know.

This is why we do missionary work—to help others know the true way to worship.

What Does This Mean to You?

It means you'll want to know how we worship in The Church of Jesus Christ of Latter-day Saints.

It means you'll be a good missionary now and share the truth you know.

It means you'll try to love all of God's children.

Learning the eleventh Article of Faith will remind you that we believe people should be able to worship the way they want to, each one according to the dictates of his or her own conscience. We claim that privilege, and we allow all men the same privilege, let them worship how, where, or what they may.

Remember, people usually do the best they can with what they know and what they have. It is a good habit to honor* people who turn to God. We can try to understand and to respect the way they worship. It is sacred to them.

To behave in any other way is unkind, unholy. It is not Christlike to laugh, scoff, or be noisy while someone else is worshiping. That goes for the people in your own ward too!

It is a good idea to live as an example of the believers in the eleventh Article of Faith: "We claim the privilege of worshiping Almighty God according to the dictates of our own conscience, and allow all men the same privilege, let them worship how, where, or what they may."

Scriptures to Study

Bible: Matthew 5:44–48; John 8:32–36
Book of Mormon: 1 Nephi 21:7; Alma 21:22

*See "What the Words Mean."

12. We believe in being subject to kings, presidents, rulers, and magistrates, in obeying, honoring, and sustaining the law.

About the Twelfth Article of Faith: Law

Since the beginning, some of God's children have made life tough for others. Cain killed Abel even though their parents, Adam and Eve, talked with God! Cain should have known better and should have kept the law.

Moses had to lead the children of Israel away from their mortal enemies, through the wilderness and across the Red Sea. They were miserable people until Moses came along. They had been subject to a variety of kings and rulers. And they had been slaves. The Ten Commandments were laws they tried to live by once they were freed.

Some early Christians were thrown into a den of lions. Spectators gathered in the great Roman colosseum and made sport of the whole tragedy. They watched, cheered, and kept score as gentle disciples of Christ were destroyed by vicious animals. These true believers did *not* wage war. They went to death singing hymns.

Christ's enemies took him before Pilate, who was the chief ruler in Jerusalem and who judged those who broke the law. Christ did not use his godly powers to overcome Pilate. He played out his own role and allowed Pilate to play his. And Jesus was crucified.

In the beginning days of the Church in this dispensation, people became angry at members of the Church because they didn't understand them. Perhaps they were stirred up and responded to promptings from Satan. They made life miserable for these early Church members. Joseph Smith had personally approached the president of the United States, and the governor, too, for help. But they gave no help. They promised no protection under the law.

In countries and cities where people are oppressed, the followers of Christ have determined to privately do what is right and publicly obey their rulers. What we are to do is work to bring about better government and better leaders in our local areas.

Movies and comic books tell about Batman as he became a hero for "cleaning up" wickedness in the make-believe metropolis of Gotham. Children watching this movie in theaters clapped and cheered when Batman overcame the political evils of the city.

Moses overcame such evils in his day. Esther in hers. Joseph of Egypt in his. Alma in his. Moroni in his. You in yours!

Remember, Jesus Christ said, "Mine house is a house of order" (D&C 132:8).

Wouldn't it be dreadful if there were no order, no respect for leaders, no proper followers, no knowledge or concern for laws and for the reasons why they are written? And what would it be like to be part of a family or go to a school or live in a community where everyone did exactly what he or she wanted? Confusion and theft would rob peace and order. It would not be pleasant. Soon there would be chaos, and that is not what heaven nor heaven on earth is about.

What Does This Mean to You?

It means that ultimately life can be better for you and your loved ones. But it means you will have to work for this in your own way.

It means that, to help ensure order, you will want to become familiar with laws that govern your family, your church, your community, and your country.

It means that you will sharpen your wit and your skills to be one who not only sustains the current law and leaders but is willing to work to improve the situation, if need be.

It is a good idea to live as an example of the believers in the twelfth Article of Faith, which states, "We believe in being subject to kings, presidents, rulers, and magistrates, in obeying, honoring, and sustaining the law."

Scriptures to Study

Bible: Exodus 22:28; Proverbs 24:21

13. We believe in being honest, true, chaste, benevolent, virtuous, and in doing good to all men; indeed, we may say that we follow the admonition of Paul—We believe all things, we hope all things, we have endured many things, and hope to be able to endure all things. If there is anything virtuous, lovely, or of good report or praiseworthy, we seek after these things.

About the Thirteenth Article of Faith:
Seek

The thirteenth Article of Faith is about seeking after the good things in life.

Do you know what it means for you *to be honest?* We're not talking about bank robberies here, though small-change stuff is probably how a bank robber gets his start.

We're talking about the kinds of things some young people do —shoplifting, "borrowing" from little brother's piggy bank, getting answers from your neighbor's paper in a school test. We're talking about lying about your age to beat theater or cafe prices and other restrictions, not admitting you broke Aunt Cathy's favorite lamp, acting innocent before Dad about the dent in the car fender, lying to your mother about where you went and with whom.

Honestly, honesty is the best policy. And as members of The Church of Jesus Christ of Latter-day Saints, we believe in being honest. Do you? Are you honest?

Do you know what it means for you *to be true?* It means to be consistent with good character. It means to be loyal and steadfast. It means to be accurate, square, dependable, and without variation. These are dictionary definitions.

What it really means is that you do what you are supposed to do (according to God's will) when you are supposed to do it.

For example, a girl named Rachel made an agreement with a neighbor, Mrs. Tanner, that she would come by each Monday to help clean the house. They settled on the amount that Rachel would be paid and the time of day she would arrive.

The first Monday was a success. Rachel came on time, worked, was paid, and promised to see Mrs. Tanner next week.

Next week Rachel *did* see Mrs. Tanner, but only long enough to say she couldn't come because she had a rehearsal at school.

The next week she came late and left early. To her credit, she wouldn't take any money because she felt a little guilty.* But that didn't help Mrs. Tanner with her housekeeping.

The next week Rachel just didn't come or call.

If Rachel had treated you that way, what would you think?

Rachel wasn't true.

Do you know what it means for you *to be chaste?* It means that you are morally clean. It means that you are innocent of unlawful sexual acts. You are pure of body and spirit. It's the right way to be for one who has been given the gift of the Holy Ghost, which can operate only with one who is clean and worthy before God.

---

*See "What the Words Mean."

Do you know what it means for you *to be benevolent?* It means that you voluntarily feed the family animals.

You take the crying baby out of the chapel.

You shovel Widow Brown's walks before you do your own —and without being told.

While the parents have an evening out, you tend the children next door—for nothing!

You open doors, tote packages, help with wraps.

You stash crumpled paper dropped in the church foyer.

You do good deeds. You help.

Do you know what it means for you *to do good to all men?* It means that you truly understand that every person who lives on earth is a child of God—not just you Mormon kids! You are trying to live more like Jesus, to be even as he is. You will be one who will help Christ in his mission to bring to pass the immortality and eternal life of all men.

Now, that is doing good!

Do you know what it means for you *to endure all things?* It means that to qualify for heaven you must make it on earth. Everyone is here to be tested. God said so, and we can read about this in the Pearl of Great Price,* Abraham 3:25. And if you can help someone else make it, so much the better.

Elder Jeffrey R. Holland has told this story about endurance and about doing good for others:

"A Church leader in an eastern city was approached by a little boy and asked to come to the boy's home, where his sister was seriously ill. Although he didn't know the boy, the older man responded immediately.

"He found the home to be a wretched one-room basement in a tenement. The mother had died, the father had disappeared, and the fifteen-year-old sister had carried on for the younger children. For almost a year she had been both breadwinner and mother, and now she lay in the terminal stages of a fatal disease.

---

*See "What the Words Mean."

"They talked that night of the future, of Heavenly Father's plan for his children, and of the joy that a homecoming would bring. The girl found warmth and peace in this Church leader's words and in their prayer, but one persistent question kept coming to her childlike mind:

" 'But *how?*' she asked. '*How* will he know that I belong to him?'

"As he prayed silently for help, the man received even as he gave. Looking down at the frail little creature, he saw on the ragged blanket the shriveled and work-worn fingers that had kept the dishes washed and the clothes ironed and the food cooked—fingers that by service and sacrifice had brought life to a little family.

" 'Show him your hands,' he said quietly. 'He'll know you belong to him.' " (Jeffrey R. Holland, "Show Him Your Hands," *Improvement Era,* October 1967, p. 39.)

Do you *know what it means to be virtuous?* President Gordon B. Hinckley once told a group of youth: "Is there a valid case for virtue? It is the only way to freedom from regret. The peace of conscience which flows therefrom is the only personal peace that is not counterfeit. And beyond all of this is the unfailing promise of God to those who walk in virtue. Declared Jesus of Nazareth, speaking on the mountain, 'Blessed are the pure in heart, for they shall see God.' That is a covenant, made by him who has the power to fulfill." (Gordon B. Hinckley, *Improvement Era*, December 1970, p. 149.)

It could seem to be increasingly harder to be virtuous in a world full of silliness, sin, and downright dangerous temptations. But you can do it. You have been given a gift within you—a gift from God! Neglect not the gift that is in you, but use it to guide and strengthen you and keep you apart from the destroying angel.

Do you *know how to be praiseworthy?* Learn about the Lord. What was he like? What did he do about temptation, heartbreak, sin, the needy? What was he good at? He was very good at forgiveness, love, patience, teaching, and obeying Heavenly Father.

Follow the Lord. Do what he did in similar situations.

Come unto Christ the Lord. Draw close to God in prayer, as Jesus did. He'll be there for you. The more you try to be like Jesus, the closer you will feel to him. The more praiseworthy you'll be.

Why do you *seek after things of good report?* Life is eternal, and you are rapidly becoming what you are going to be forever. You need to know good things.

Life is too long to be involved with shabby things, immoral things, anti-Christ things. Life is too short not to seek out books, music, movies, activities, studies, work, and friends that lift you and shape you well.

You are what you eat. You are what you think. You are what you program into your sensitive mind. Your spirit responds the way it is nurtured too.

What Does This Mean to You?

It means that you are blessed to be a member of The Church of Jesus Christ of Latter-day Saints.

It means you have precious perspective of life and life eternal.

It means you are provided with programs to help you grow according to God's will for you.

It means you receive ordinances and opportunities to be enriched spiritually.

It means you have more the advantage because you have been given the gift of the Holy Ghost.

It means that you understand and value relationships: with God, with family, with choice friends, and with other Church members.

It means that you awaken to the responsibility that is yours to be charitable, helpful, and serving to others who aren't so fortunate as you.

It means you should be grateful, faithful, and joyful!

It means that it is a good idea to live as "an example of the believers, in word, in conversation, in charity, in spirit, in faith, in purity" (1 Timothy 4:12).

Scriptures to Study

Bible: James 1:27; Matthew 7:12
Doctrine and Covenants 132:52

5

About Persisting

You have persisted* through this book. You are terrific!

So what if somebody *made* you read it!

Or maybe somebody read it to you.

Maybe your teacher taught the principles in Primary or Sunday School.

Maybe, happily, you struck out on your own and decided to read for yourself this birthday-present book written especially for you.

However you got *here,* if you have come this far you have persisted. And that's good. You just can't spend time studying gospel principles without benefit to your life. You'll get more out of seminary, Young Women, Aaronic Priesthood assignments. You should care about yourself and your life enough by now to know

---

*See "What the Words Mean."

why you are participating in these opportunities the Church provides.

You'll have a better chance of keeping your covenants through the dating years. Covenants? Remember? Each time you take the sacrament you promise to always remember the Lord Jesus and to keep his commandments—which include absolute moral purity, obeying the Word of Wisdom, faithfully praying, and serving the Lord by doing good to others. And it doesn't mean "someday." It means now.

You'll be better prepared for a full-time mission, the temple endowment, and marriage someday not *too* far away.

Turning twelve, guided by the thirteen Articles of Faith, puts you up front in personal progress. Persisting can make it really happen. Success in life is more than talk.

What follows below is some personal writing from the journal of a bright young marathon runner. Running a marathon is a very big undertaking, and the parallel to life is interesting. Think about yourself and your personal progress as you read Tony's feelings.

"During the 1970s in the United States, running became an extremely popular form of exercise. All over the country, runners signed up for races of various distances, some designed to test primarily speed, others designed to test primarily endurance. The premier endurance test is the marathon.

"The marathon traces its roots back to classical Greece. In 490 B.C., the Persians under King Darius attacked Greece. The main force attacked at the plain of Marathon, some twenty-five miles from Athens. Although badly outnumbered, the Greeks managed to beat the invading armies back to their ships. A solitary warrior, exhausted from battle, nonetheless ran the distance back to Athens to bring the welcome news to those at home. There he gasped out his final words, 'Rejoice, we conquer!'

"This remarkable effort was memorialized by Olympic races, and is still the distance of our modern marathons. Now the term *marathon* has broadened to include any contest or activity of great length that requires unusual effort and endurance.

"Marathon runners know why this is so. They will explain that the race is half over only when you have run at least twenty miles, not thirteen. Although twenty miles seems incredibly long to the rest of us, most well-prepared marathon runners find they can run that distance without too much trouble. It is the remaining six miles or so that make the marathon such a test of human endurance. Many runners experience what they call 'hitting the wall'—an almost sudden urge to quit, a nearly tangible obstacle that requires a tremendous effort to hurdle.

"I recently ran my first marathon. I set my goal several months in advance, and disciplined myself to follow the rigorous training schedule. I sought advice from more experienced runners, and read what guidebooks I could find. I carefully increased my total mileage each week. Running too far too soon could bring on an injury.

"Finally the day of the marathon arrived. I had set a goal for a finishing time of three hours and fifteen minutes: a time that was realistic, if all went well. This was the culmination of months of training, discipline, and sacrifice. About eight miles into the race, on a downhill part of the course, I passed Brent, an older runner who had given me helpful advice during previous training runs when we would find ourselves on a similar course at the same time.

"Brent had run dozens of marathons, and was a strong and steady runner. As I ran by him, Brent said, 'I'll see you again later.' Then I remembered the stories Brent and others had told me about athletes who start too fast, and then are 'finished' before the race is. Inexperienced runners are especially tempted to push too hard on the downhill portions of the course. The easiness is deceptive, for the sharp downgrades are tougher on the muscles and joints than are the upgrades. So I decided to match my stride to Brent's disciplined and experienced one.

"As we came out of the canyon to pass the eighteen-mile mark, I struggled to stay with Brent. 'I want to have someone with me when I am hitting the wall,' I explained. We began to encounter spectators along the road, who cheered us on. This gave us a boost I hadn't expected. In gratitude I tried to thank or wave to them all.

"For over two more miles I kept pace with Brent, and then I felt the sudden loss of energy, the almost overwhelming desire to stop and walk that characterizes 'hitting the wall.'

" 'Stay with me,' Brent encouraged. 'We all experience it at some point, but you can get through it. Stay with me and I'll help pull you through.' I also knew that my wife and children and other family members would be waiting almost a mile ahead. Drawing on the strength provided by these thoughts, I was able to hang on until the desire to quit passed for a time.

"I was surprised how the cheers of my family spurred me on. It seemed to give Brent a boost, too, that carried him forward while my family drove past in the car to stop another mile down the course. There again, the encouraging cheers of my family provided a much-needed lift that helped both of us ignore the fatigue. I was glad that I had thus been able to return Brent's earlier help.

"A little later, sensing that I was withdrawing inward, where I might focus on the pain and exhaustion, Brent urged, 'Don't give in to it. I am beat, too. Even the winning runners feel the pain. We're getting close, though, and you're doing great.'

"The final two miles of this marathon follow Salt Lake's Days of '47 parade route. We could now see the crowds lining the streets in anticipation of the parade. 'I know you want to be friendly and are grateful for the cheers,' Brent cautioned, 'but I have found that you have to conserve every ounce of strength from here on in. I only wave back if someone I know calls my name. That's a hint from lots of experience.' So I wisely followed the advice, conserved my strength, and found that Brent was right —I needed every bit of strength for the end of the race.

"I was surprised that the last mile was the hardest of all. Running slightly uphill and facing the rising sun, I now felt thoroughly spent. I began counting blocks, which passed in slow motion, seeming more like miles.

"As the finish line came into view, Brent said, 'Take me in, buddy, pull me in.'

"Challenged by this last chance to return a little of the help I had received, I felt a sudden spring of energy, and poured on the speed to pull my partner in.

"We crossed the finish line just five seconds apart. Exhausted far beyond anything I had ever experienced, I was nevertheless elated to know that I had beaten my goal by over fifteen minutes, and had finished among the top twenty-five runners.

"I would never have done so well without Brent. I am not sure whether I would have been able to finish. Brent's concern and encouragement, together with the knowledge that he had experienced it before, pulled me through." (Anthony J. Cannon, September 1989.)

When we happen to be in the stage of life in which we are turning twelve or more, it is good to have examples of the believers to follow; heroes and heroines to learn from. President Spencer W. Kimball is such an example.

When he was about your age, or maybe younger, he was a great help to his father around their farm. He did all the chores that boys and strong girls are so good at—gathering and stomping hay, hoeing the vegetable garden, feeding the chickens, and milking the cows.

He was a lively young man and enjoyed doing those chores that kept him moving about. But milking the cows was boring. And it had to be done every day, no matter what.

Sometimes Spencer felt like a slave to those cows.

One day he decided he was going to have to do something about it. The fact was that the cows had to be milked. That could only be done sitting on a stool, working at the job until it was done. There ought to be something he could do along with the milking that would make the time pass faster and that would bring some pleasure to the task. Like singing!

So he sang. And he sang.

He propped up a hymnbook and learned all the words to all the hymns that he especially enjoyed. He tried to study the musical notes as he memorized the words to the hymns, because Spencer played the piano too. He was popular with friends because he knew so many songs and had such joy in singing. As he traveled the world as a Church leader, he often entertained the Saints by accompanying himself as he sang. At parties the General Authorities of the Church had, Spencer W. Kimball organized singing groups among the Brethren such as Harold B. Lee and Marion G. Romney. He was glad he'd learned so many songs.

Another thing he did when he was milking the cows was to memorize scriptures. There was plenty of time. And if a fellow had to sit there, he might as well make it time well spent.

Some days he'd lean a copy of the Book of Mormon or the Bible against a big rock on a barrel. That way he could read the scriptures and not even notice that he was milking! It was wonderful.

Of course, his friends and family were impressed at the persistence of this young man, and many suggested that those cows knew more about the gospel than a lot of folks who sat in the church on Sunday.

You may not have to milk cows, but you can find ways to persist in your efforts to grow closer to the Lord, to keep all of his commandments, to grow in knowledge and spirit, and to seek after the good, praiseworthy things in life. You can. You can!

As President Spencer W. Kimball would say, "Do it!"

6

What the Words Mean

Aaronic Priesthood: known as the lesser priesthood because it is a preparation for the greater priesthood or the Melchizedek Priesthood.* Those who faithfully hold the Aaronic Priesthood are in a position to have angels minister to them and are of special assistance to the ward bishop, and as priests are authorized to baptize by immersion. A young man is eligible for this priesthood at the age of twelve. (See Doctrine and Covenants section 13.)

Anoint: to apply oil to the head (of a sick person, for example) in preparation for blessing the person.

Apostasy: departure from the true gospel of Jesus Christ. Churchwide apostasy began not long after Christ's crucifixion and

---

*See "What the Words Mean."

95

continued to develop when his original Apostles were killed off. The loss of the gospel truth brought about the Dark Ages, when people's minds were without the light of God.

Apostle: one called to be a special witness of Christ and to serve in the perfecting of the Saints, the work of the ministry, and the "edifying of the body of Christ" (see Ephesians 4:12).

Articles of Faith: thirteen statements Joseph Smith made that summarize many of the basic doctrines of the Church. They were given in response to a request by a Mr. Wentworth about what Church members believed.

Atonement: the great sacrifice Jesus Christ made when he took all the sins of mankind upon himself and by his death and resurrection brought all of us the resurrection. The Atonement is the foundation upon which all gospel principles rest; it was necessary because of the fall of Adam and Eve. To atone is to redeem, to pay the price or penalty for; it is the way of bringing mankind back into the presence of God.

Authority: power to influence because of position or education; a person cited as an expert.

Baptism for the dead: baptism of a living person on behalf of one who died without this saving ordinance.

Bestow: to give; to convey as a gift.

Bishop: in the Church, head of members in a geographical area known as a ward; one having priesthood authority and ordained to be a common judge in Israel.

Book of Mormon: sacred scripture recorded prior to A.D. 421; an abridged account of God's children in ancient America, translated from metal plates by Joseph Smith as part of the restoration of the gospel; another witness for Jesus Christ, with the doctrines of salvation clear and complete.

Called: in the religious sense, to be picked by God or those inspired by him to serve in a particular office or assignment.

Choice: a selection; a decision or preference between at least two options.

Condemnation: blame, censure, act of condemning; act of damning or declaring wrong.

Consecrated oil: olive oil that has been dedicated or set apart to be used in the anointing of the sick. Oil thus consecrated should not be used for any other purpose.

Consequences: results of following a set of conditions, acts, choices.

Covenant: a sacred promise; an agreement between two or more persons that each will do certain things.

Crucified: killed by being nailed on a cross. Crucifixion is an excruciating way to die. Prophets foretold that the method of death for Christ would be crucifixion. After his resurrection Christ showed the nail wounds on his hands and feet. (See 3 Nephi 11:14– 29; Luke 24:36.)

Deity: a god; supreme being.

Dictates: commands, instructions.

Doctrine: religious teaching, principles.

Eternal life: celestial life forever; the kind of life Heavenly Father and Jesus live.

Evangelist: an ordained patriarch.

Faith: first principle of the gospel. "Faith is the assurance which men have of the existence of things which they have not seen," according to the Prophet Joseph Smith (*Lectures on Faith*).

Fast: to go without food and drink for a period of time while drawing close to the Lord. A true fast is accompanied by prayer or, as it says in the scripture, "rejoicing and prayer" (D&C 59:14).

Free agency: the God-given right each person has to make his or her own choices between good and evil.

General conference: a meeting for the worldwide membership of the Church, held twice a year in April and October in the Salt Lake Tabernacle, for the purpose of lifting the Saints, worshiping the Lord, and reporting on the status of the Church.

Glory: beauty and splendor.

Godhead: the three exalted Beings, Heavenly Father, his Son Jesus Christ, and the Holy Ghost.

God's will: what he wants; what is pleasing to him.

Gospel: the message concerning Christ, the kingdom of God, and salvation for mankind. The gospel includes ordinances as well as doctrine.

Guilt: self-reproach; spiritual unrest before God; lack of peace; extreme discomfort for personal offenses. To relieve guilt requires repentance or changing one's ways.

Heavenly Father: the Father of our spirits. We used to live in heaven with him, and we hope to return to live with him again. We pray to him in the name of Jesus Christ.

Holy Ghost: third member of the Godhead; a spirit being who does not have a body of flesh and bones as do Jesus and Heavenly Father; the Comforter, the Revelator, the messenger of the Father and the Son. Having his companionship is a great gift bestowed at the time of confirmation following baptism. The gifts of the Holy Ghost include prophecies, visions, speaking in tongues, etc.

Honor: to show esteem, recognition; to treat with respect, as in "honor thy father and thy mother."

Immortality: unending, everlasting life.

Israel: literally means "contender with God" or "one who has succeeded before God." Jacob, son of Isaac, who was son of Abraham of old, was called Israel, Prince of God. His sons and their families and posterity became known as the children of Israel.

Jesus Christ: Heavenly Father's Only Begotten Son in the flesh; the Redeemer; the God of this earth, born of Mary in Bethlehem.

Kingdom of God on earth: at this time, The Church of Jesus Christ of Latter-day Saints. In the kingdom of God on earth, there must be a prophet, priesthood authority, and continued revelation from God to his leaders.

Laying on of hands: the placing of the hands of the Lord's authorized servants on a person's head in order to bestow blessings, ordinations, callings, anointings, and so on, according to the order of God. You can read about part of this in Mark 16:18.

Lineage: ancestry by blood or adoption. Elder Bruce R. McConkie wrote, "As inheritors of the blessings of Jacob, it is the privilege of the gathered remnant of Jacob to receive their own patriarchal blessings and, by faith, to be blessed equally with the ancients" (*Mormon Doctrine* [Salt Lake City: Bookcraft, 1966], p.

558). An ordained patriarch may also declare a person's lineage in the tribes of Israel, declaring him to be of the tribe of Ephraim, etc.

Literal: exact; verbatim; according to the facts.

Melchizedek Priesthood: the higher or greater priesthood; the power and keys to all spiritual blessings of the Church. Named for the great high priest in ancient times to avoid too frequent repetition of the name of Deity, this priesthood's full name is the Holy Priesthood after the Order of the Son of God.

Millennium: means a thousand years, just as a hundred years is a century. In the gospel, we refer to the Millennium as that time of peace when the earth will be renewed and made as beautiful as paradise, and when Christ will personally reign on earth.

Miracles: "In the broadest sense, miracles embrace all those events which are beyond the power of any presently known physical power to produce" (Bruce R. McConkie, *Mormon Doctrine,* p. 506).

Missionaries: each of us who has been given the gift of the Holy Ghost and who has covenanted with Christ at baptism is a missionary with the responsibility to spread understanding about the Savior and his restored church. Formally, the term *missionaries* refers to men and women from late teens to senior citizens in age who, for a period of time, leave their regular life to proselyte (or search out and teach) those who are ready to covenant with Christ to do his will and work. They do so at their own expense.

Mummy: a dead body, treated for burial in a special way after the manner of ancient Egyptians, so as to preserve it.

New Jerusalem: Latter-day revelation tells us that a New Jerusalem will be built in Jackson County, Missouri, where Saints will dwell at the time of the Millennium.

Ordained: given authority in the priesthood by the laying on of hands by God's appointed servants.

Ordinance: something decreed by deity and formalized in a ceremony, such as baptism, a healing blessing, marriage, or the temple endowment.

Papyri: scrolls made of papyrus plants flattened into a kind of paper.

Paradisiacal: like the Garden of Eden; similar to paradise.

Patriarch: a man who speaks for the Lord as he lays his hands on the head of a worthy individual member of the Church. He tells of blessings in store for him (or her), gives special guidelines for his life's mission, and declares his lineage.

Patriarchal blessing: a blessing given by a patriarch and recorded in Church archives. A recommend is required to obtain a patriarchal blessing. A father, who is a natural patriarch, may give a father's blessing to his children.

Pearl of Great Price: a volume of scripture containing some of Joseph Smith's translations and writings.

Persist: keep going; endure; never give up.

Pilgrim: one of faith who travels to a holy place, a shrine, a church; one who makes a journey to a foreign land for religious reasons.

Plan of life (plan of salvation): the plan given to us by Heavenly Father and implemented by Jesus Christ, a plan which trains us, gives us opportunities to gain knowledge and to increase in spirituality, and has as its goal preparation for exaltation or eternal life.

Primitive church: the Church as it was organized in the time of Christ and under his direction.

Privilege: special benefit.

Prophet: the Twelve Apostles and the members of the First Presidency of the Church are prophets, seers, and revelators; but the President of the Church is considered "the prophet" and the ultimate authority on earth to receive God's direction for the Church.

Repent: to turn about, change course, cease sinning; to ask God's forgiveness; to feel sorrow for one's sins and to forsake them.

Restoration: the act of making whole again; bringing something back as it was. The restoration of the gospel of Jesus Christ began with the vision of Joseph Smith and continued with the organization of the Church in 1830 and the bringing back of the ordinances and teachings of the ancient Church.

Resurrection: the raising of the physical body from the grave and its being reunited forever with its spirit body.

Revelation: the communication of divine truth, such as messages from God through his appointed leaders, for the benefit of man.

Sacrament: an ordinance of the gospel of Jesus Christ. The sacrament of bread and water is taken in remembrance of the flesh and blood of Jesus Christ, who sacrificed his life for us. You may read in Moroni 4:1–3 and 5:1–2 the sacramental prayers that Christ gave to the ancient Nephite people, which we also use today.

Sacred: holy; of God; worthy to be treated with reverence.

Scriptures: the word of God that he has revealed to his prophets, printed in at least four books—the Bible (Old and New

Testaments), the Book of Mormon, the Doctrine and Covenants, and the Pearl of Great Price.

Sealing: binding, bonding, making permanent; sealing of ordinances by Holy Spirit of Promise, based on faithfulness.

Second Coming: that time when Christ will come to earth again to live and will personally reign on earth in glory, known to all men. The first coming of Jesus was the time when he was born to Mary in Bethlehem and completed that portion of his mission which included the events surrounding the Atonement, the Crucifixion, and the Resurrection.

Soul: the eternal entity of spirit within the human body. After resurrection the spirit and body will be inseparable, making an immortal being.

Spiritual gifts: personal abilities and powers which follow the obedient and faithful; powers to do things beyond natural ability; talents enhanced by God. In 1 Corinthians 12:31, the faithful are reminded to desire and seek spiritual gifts.

Ten tribes: the twelve tribes are the posterity of Israel, or Jacob, the followers and family of his twelve sons, named for them. Ten of the twelve tribes were scattered anciently because they forsook God.

Three witnesses: Oliver Cowdery, David Whitmer, and Martin Harris. These three associates of Joseph Smith were given the privilege of seeing the plates from which the Book of Mormon was translated, and hearing the voice of the Lord. (See introductory pages of the Book of Mormon, "The Testimony of the Three Witnesses.")

Tongues: speaking in tongues or translating them for the spiritual growth of those in the kingdom of God on earth. Speaking in tongues might be a speech in the pure language of God as a manifestation of his Spirit, or a special understanding for a period of time of a foreign language in order to help do the work of the Lord.

Transgressions: sins, violations of the law.

Urim and Thummim: an instrument prepared by God to assist man in gaining revelation from the Lord and to help in translating records written in unknown languages.

Verily: truthfully; refers to something spoken or written in honesty.

Visions: instances in which people, through the blessing of the Spirit, are permitted to see beyond their natural ability. Visions and revelations are always found in the true Church.

Witness: one who gives proof or swears evidence; one who makes public affirmation of a religious belief or happening.

Zion: God's people have always been known as Zion; also a place of God; a feeling for God in the heart; utopia; homeland for the children of Israel.